Entrance to the Alchemical Amphitheatre

A Six-Module Introductory Course of Magickal Alchemy in the Path of Salt

by Marcus Katz M.A. (Western Esotericism)

Published by FORGE PRESS 2008
"Books for the Enquiring Mind"
1 Wood Cottages, Keswick, Cumbria CA12 4NT, England
www.forgepress.com

ISBN 978-0-9558566-0-0

Copyright © Marcus Katz, 2008

An Alchemical Blessing

Cabala and Alchemy
Give thee the medicine most high.
Also the Stone of the Wise,
In which alone the foundation lies,
As is plain before thine eyes
Betimes in these effigies.

O God help us to be grateful
For this gift sublime and pure
The man whose heart and mind Thou openest,
Who is perfect herein
To prepare here this Work
To him may all strength be given.[*]

---

[*] Steffan Michelspacher, *Cabala* (1616), Cabala, mirror of Art and Nature: in Alchemy

About the Author

In 2007, Marcus Katz became the first student in the world to complete the M.A. in Western esotericism at the prestigious University of Exeter. He has been immersed in the practical and academic study of esotericism for over thirty years, and now teaches Witchcraft, Ritual, Kabbalah, Tarot and Alchemy at the Far Away Centre in the beautiful Lake District of England. His professional approach to the subject is strengthened by his M.B.A.

Marcus is currently engaged in PhD Research into the teachings of Western esoteric orders of the late 18th century. His work and research takes him around the world; he has traveled across Egypt several times, performing rituals, taught Inner Guide Meditations and Kabbalah in Switzerland, and worked extensively in the US and Asia-Pacific.

Marcus is a member of SHAC, the Society for the History of Alchemy and Chemistry, and ESSWE, the European Society for the Study of Western Esotericism. He is the Chairman of Tarot Professionals, a member of ATA, the American Tarot Association and the Tarot Guild of Australia.

As a licensed NLP trainer and Hypnotherapist, he is interested in providing different and effective learning experiences for his students and clients, and often produces innovative methods, such as his Tarot in Ten Minutes, or in this course, the Coagula Cocktail!

His Kabbalah course is available through the popular Magicka School, in addition to a mentored option on his own website. He also offers a unique **apprenticeship scheme** which covers the entire initiatory work of Magick for selected personal students. If you want to learn real Magick, beyond Harry Potter and "the Secret", a real apprenticeship course awaits you now.

To contact Marcus and for course details: http://www.farawaycentre.com

This present Alchemy course is also available as a download through Magicka School, http://www.magickaschool.com and as a paperback book through http://www.forgepress.com. Students are recommended to purchase the paperback for ease of recording results and making reference.

Table of Contents

Course Structure	6
Reading List	8
Website and Links	9
Introduction	10
Module 1: Calcination	14
Module 2: Solution	38
Module 3: Separation	54
Module 4: Conjunction	69
Module 5: Putrefaction	91
Module 6: Coagulation	111
Bibliography & Reading List	123
Notes	125
Index	136

Structure of the Amphitheatre Course

This six-module course is designed to give you an *introduction* to the art and science of magical alchemy. Each module has been structured to give you a variety of activities, to ensure that whatever your learning style you'll get the most opportunity to experience the teachings of Alchemy and use them to enrich your daily life.

The content of each module is sufficient for a month of study, meditation and practice, although further reading is provided if you wish to extend your studies at any stage during or after the course.

Each of the six modules has six sections, which relate to the overall subject of the module. There are three *readings*; these provide background material and specific information on alchemical subjects, such as an element like *Sulpher*, or a character like *Paracelsus*. These begin with general subjects to introduce you to Alchemy, and progress to deeper issues as you become more comfortable with the material. The three readings of each module are one of each; general; academic; and an extract from source material; so that you can choose which - or all - suit your interest.

Each module has also three further elements; *Techne*, *Praxis* and *Theoria*. These are three different ways to learn more about the subject of the module. You can try one, two or all three of the approaches!

The first, *techne*, is a productive approach - you will try an alchemical experiment to learn about the relationship of alchemy to your real life!

The second, *praxis*, is a meditative approach - by working with your imagination and the powerful symbolism of alchemy you will enrich your appreciation of the world of Nature through alchemy. You may find this also creates magical changes in your environment that cannot be explained!

The third approach is *theoria* - this is your chance to think about your reading and experience, create an essay, making sense of alchemy in your own mind.

The readings for this course are based on academic research and are therefore factual to primary or secondary source materials. They are also extensively annotated. As such, they require careful reading and you may have to re-visit the material many times! Although this is an introduction to Alchemy, it is also deliberately dense in material which has been thoroughly reviewed. This is in order to dispel many of the second-hand writings on the subject which place Alchemy as originating in Atlantis or similar ideas.

All of the practical material in this course is unique, and has been constructed for this course alone. You will not find these rituals, exercises or meditations anywhere else on the internet or in publication. The material herein is the result of two years research, and the exercises the result of thirty years practice.

You will also appreciate that even this course structure is alchemical - divided into six modules reflecting the first six stages of the alchemical process. It is hoped you will be able to generalize these teachings to all areas of your experience, in order to live a truly magical - and alchemically transformative - life! Some of these apparently simple exercises and ideas, delivered and followed in the right order, can have profound and challenging impact on your perspective, state of consciousness and external life.

As an introduction to Magickal Alchemy, the practical experiments here concentrate on the usage of Salt, rather than Sulpher or Mercury, for reasons of safety. Also, salt is a commonplace item that may easily be purchased and is likely to already be present in your home! We will see how the mundane and commonplace may be utilized by the alchemist and turned into a deep teaching of the nature of Universe† and further magically transform your relationship to it.

Please note that all experiments suggested here are carried out at your own risk and should be treated with a degree of respect. Although seemingly straightforward, even mundane, the work of Alchemy can have profoundly positive yet challenging effects.

---

† I use the term 'Universe' rather than 'the Universe' to denote the comprehensiveness of the word.

Reading List

This course is intended to be self-contained and studied stand-alone to any other material. However, the following titles are invaluable and highly recommended:

- Stanislas Klossowski de Rola, *The Golden Game*
- E. J. Holmyard, *Alchemy*
- Edward F. Edinger, *Anatomy of the Psyche*
- S. J. Linden, *The Alchemy Reader*

These are also listed and available through the Far Away Centre site, amongst many other recommended books on Tarot, Kabbalah, Witchcraft and Ritual.

There is also a comprehensive reading list at the end of this course for your further study.

Websites and Links

The most comprehensive selection of writings and images on Alchemy is on Adam McLean's Alchemy site at:

http://www.levity.com/alchemy/home.html

You may also wish to pursue your study of Kabbalah, Witchcraft and Tarot in workshops and classes at the Far Away Centre:

http://www.farawaycentre.com

And on-line Kabbalah Courses, Witchcraft and Tarot courses at Magicka School:

http://www.magickaschool.com

Introduction: A New Perspective on Alchemy

The Alchemist in his Workshop, David Teniers (1610-1690)

What is Magickal Alchemy?

There are many ideas about the source and meaning of the word Alchemy, with some claiming it comes from the Arabic, al-khem, meaning the "Art of the land of Khem" (Egypt, Khem means 'Black') or the "art of transformation".

The word may also derive from the Greek, meaning "the alloying of metals," and it is common knowledge that the principle aim of its practitioners was to turn lead into gold, or create an elixir bestowing eternal life. Other writers, particularly the psychotherapist C.G. Jung (1875 - 1961), delve deeper into the art, noting that the chemical transformations and strange diagrams of kings in baths and ravens in bedrooms can be taken as emblems of spiritual transformation or psychological development. Another form of Alchemy, *Spagyric* Alchemy, concentrates on vegetable and plant work, making elixirs and tinctures.

In this course, we concentrate on the nature of Alchemy as a magical and transformative practice, with initiatory, ritual and mystical implications.

The various stages described by some alchemists of turning lead into gold are here seen as an initiatory system describing and foreshadowing the steps of moving from a mundane life to a mystical one. It is in this context we will explore alchemy, particularly in providing exercises which will encourage you to look at the relationship between yourself and Universe through natural processes of transformation.

You will also see how your own work contributes to the transformation of the "one thing" described by Alchemy - the Philosopher's Stone which is Universe.

A Personal Story of Alchemy

When I first started to study alchemy I wanted to look at the building blocks of the alchemical system, which are the chemicals and metals. I decided to find a common alchemical material each month, and make notes as to its significance, both alchemical and mundane, and then at the end of the year perform an Alchemical Mass involving all the twelve materials.

I began with salt, and placed some in a dish by my bed. As the days passed, the salt obviously began to draw moisture out of the air. As I observed the water collecting in the bowl, I began to think of the process as a means of bringing out into the open what previously existed in the atmosphere without any sign. Once this property had been noted, I not only began to observe areas in my life where a similar drawing-out was taking place, but more dramatic events of this nature unfolded, culminating in a significant change to my life. Once the month was over, I placed the resultant saltwater in a test-tube and moved onto another basic element, sand.

It was during my work with sand that I began to see another view of Alchemy. I had spent the month looking for some sand in my daily life, to place in a bowl - as I had done with the salt. My first opportunity came when I was asked to get some sand and grit to put around a new plant my wife wanted to put in the garden. I was also told by a friend where to find a discarded bag of sand near a building site. Unfortunately, this first search revealed nothing. A week later, I was at a garage, filling the car with diesel, when I noticed a bucket of sand, obviously used to cover up fuel spills on the forecourt. I began thinking that it seemed odd that a material here could also be used for something entirely different - there is little connection between covering up slippery petrol and planting roses.

This thought progressed to the question of "why did I want sand at this moment, and not something else?" Obviously, I wanted sand for the garden. Again, "Why?" And again, so the garden looks nice. "Why?" So that I can sit in it and enjoy it. "Why?" And so forth. As the thought cascaded, I began to realise that all of us, all of the time, are collecting and redistributing various materials through the process of our lives in order to fulfill our ambitions. This is Alchemy. The Magician realizes that there is a hidden causality in all things, so their alchemy takes advantage of the hidden qualities of Nature. This is *Magickal Alchemy*, which you will be studying.

What does an Alchemist Do?

Given that we are all practicing our own alchemy, what makes a good Alchemist? Quite simply, if you want to be a good Alchemist, you need to apply a consistent and comprehensive perspective to your work with the materials in your environment. That is to say, you need to ensure that everything you are working with is contributing to your aims, and nothing is distracting you or providing an obstacle to those aims. This is known as *purification* and *consecration* in the esoteric systems; the removal of all things not required for the magical act, and the active dedication of what remains to the aim in mind.

Then, like building blocks, you need to ensure that all the materials work together, work in a sequence, and will produce the aims you have in mind.

Here are some examples of the *compounds* of this perspective of alchemy;

- A career or choice of (un)employment.
- A relationship
- A home
- A family
- A religion

Here are some examples of the *elements* from this viewpoint;

- Yourself
- Time
- A Book
- Food
- An Emotion

And finally, some of the Alchemical *transformations* undertook in this manner;

- Turning Time into Food (i.e., spending three days working for money which is exchanged for food)

- Adding Yourself, Someone Else, and Food to create a Relationship (going out for a meal with a friend)

- Turning jealousy into a rug (perhaps by acknowledging jealousy as unrecognized desire to accomplish oneself what someone else has done, in this example, a really excellent rag rug)

There are obviously a great deal many more comparisons to be made once we begin to apply Alchemical as a link between our aims of transcendence and our lives in the material world. It becomes all too clear that we often collect elements in our *Athanor*, or mixing pot, that spoil the overall mixture so that we have to tip everything out and start again.

Experimentation, as always, is the key, and the maintaining of this perspective throughout the work - what is it I am trying to achieve, and what materials am I using to achieve it? This is *Magickal Alchemy*.

Hendrick Heerschop, The Alchemist's Experiment Takes Fire, 1687

Module 1: Calcination

Calcination is the burning away by a gentle heat of impurities. In this first module, our learning aim is to burn away obsolete ideas about alchemy. We will also use our questions and work to create a gentle fire which will be maintained throughout the course. As one alchemist wrote, "give not up on Calcination!" It is important in all works of transformation to maintain a steady energy, and not burn out at the beginning or never create enough enthusiasm to gain results.

Throughout this course you may choose your route in each module, perhaps by reviewing the reading materials, performing the *praxis*, or the *techne* experiment, and then returning to the reading. You might then attempt the theoria exercise. You might prefer to run through the whole course by doing the sequence of *praxis* meditations, and only then returning to the readings or chemical *techne* experiments. The course has been written to provide a series of alchemical avenues through which you may explore the same garden and yet make it your own.

Reading 1a (Academic): Alchemy as the Asana of the West

If Kabbalah is deemed the Yoga of the West[1], then Alchemy can be considered its Asana[2] – an attitudinal position grounded in the physical world as exemplar of the divine. In the flasks, alembics, and furnaces of the laboratory, and the two-bodied lions, bathing kings and mystic mountains of the emblematic engravings, alchemy provides the esoteric tradition a phenomenology that, like *mercurius*, is both interface, synthesis and universal solvent to the particularly humanist and polyphasic concerns of the esoteric tradition.[3] It is arguable as to its significance within the esoteric tradition as a whole; although as the scholar Antoine Faivre argues, "any esoteric way passes necessarily through an alchemical ascesis, to be distinguished from asceticism."[4]

Although any definition of Alchemy is an etic construct (outsider point of view), it could be suggested that Alchemy's primary significance is in providing a testament to a western tradition – apparently scientific – and approach to esotericism in all its phases.[5] Faivre continues, "we are indeed heirs of a tradition that is specific ... whose knowledge can persuade us that the western mentality is not necessarily condemned to the roving of a spirit lacking a wisdom, which the orient alone would possess."[6]

Alchemy is concerned with both exterior and interior, hence the acronymic motto; VITRIOL, Visita Interiora Terrae Rectificando Invenies Occultum Lapidem which translates to: "Visit the interior of the earth by rectification you will find the hidden stone". In this it is identical to Asana, which is not merely physical position of the body[7], but the inherently associated and corresponding change in awareness that comes from physical changes;

> The word asana is derived from the Sanskrit verb 'Aas' which means existence and state of existence is Asana or Position. Here the position of Body as well as Mind is expected in Asana.[8]

Thus Alchemy provides the western tradition a remarkable 'referential corpus' embodying the tradition, not in a merely static way, but a dynamic process - nourishing it and feeding from it in a series of transmissions across the elements of the tradition.

It is not just the spiritual realm to which Alchemy significantly provides a bridge, but the psychological realm. Jung wrote, "Alchemy, therefore, has performed for me the great and invaluable service of providing material in which my experience could find sufficient room."[9]

The image of the alchemist as a solitary seeker, yet part of a great tradition, experimenting and discovering matters not known to the common person, makes of him a western shaman, a bridge - in themselves - between the worlds. According to Matthews, "Alchemy virtually became the equivalent of the Tantric and Varjayana path of the West."[10]

Ponce suggests three dialects, or approaches to Alchemy; psychological, mythological, and metaphysical, and we can also seek to examine the myth of the alchemist within the esoteric tradition, and its significance in the telling of the tradition itself.[11] As Norton wrote,

> "Also they wrote not every man to teach
> But to show themselves by secret speech.
> [...]
> Whereby each of his fellows were made certain:
> how that he was to them a brother,
> For every of them understood another."[12]

In this we get a hint of a secret brotherhood, much like the Rosicrucians, whose manifestos included the 'Chymical Wedding', one of the most significant allegorical tales of the initiatory system published, and significant in maintaining the myth of the Rosicrucians since its publication in 1616, following the *Fama* and *Confessio* manifestos in the prior years.

Mclean suggests that this alchemical work embodies the Rosicrucianism that

> is the esoteric philosophy lying at the heart of Western Hermeticism which provides a path for the balancing and integration of the masculine and feminine aspects of our souls, and the inner meeting of the lofty intellect with the primal earthy energies at the centre of our being.[13]

Alchemy can be seen as significantly providing the esoteric tradition;

1. An allegorical language
2. A physical exemplar of hidden (occult) processes through mimesis
3. An interface to physical sciences and the scientific method
4. An interface to Art
5. A Mystical Cosmology
6. A representation of the dynamic Psyche

As Gerry Gilchrist notes, "the Alchemist is described as the artist who, through his operations, brings nature to perfection."[14] We will consider the idea of perfecting nature later in this course, as the Work of Alchemy in either its chemical or spiritual guise is a direct correspondence to the basis of Gnostic and Esoteric models, i.e. that matter is a fallen substance or imperfect, and the virtue of man is such that it is within his remit to complete the *magnum opus* or Great Work of Creation.

Alchemy begins with its own ontology, or classification of entities. As a structure, albeit as fragmented as Gnostic ideas, with no sense of a truly monolithic foundation, it provides a framework for any creative activity. Bonus of Ferrara considered Alchemy as "the key of all good things, the Art of Art, the Science of Science,"[15] This would account for the number of "Alchemy of ..." titles in any New Age bookshop, whether it be the "Alchemy of Relationships" or "The Alchemy of All-Weather Racing."

Reading 1b (General): Alchemy and the Western Esoteric Tradition

The introduction of Alchemy to the western tradition can be precisely dated to 11th February, 1144, when Robert of Chester's "Book of the Composition of Alchemy" was published. This book was part of a new current of free-thinkers, bringing Islamic thought to the West, such as Adelard of Bath. As such, alchemy was already proving significant in cross-fertilising philosophies between east and west. Alchemy was also a publishing endeavour; "more books on alchemy were published in England between 1650 and 1680 than before or afterwards," leading to alchemy's significance as a 'public face' of esoteric workers, although the reality would differ from the stereotype.

Many such authors were Monks, such as George Ripley, an Augustine Canon. Western alchemy was often intertwined with Christian thought, comparing Christian doctrine to chemical processes. This began in the 14th century with Petrus Bonus[16] and continued throughout the 15th-17th centuries in the development of theosophical alchemy. It was only in the Victorian resurgence of alchemical idealism that a wider 'spiritual' gloss was applied to alchemy as a whole; pre-18th century alchemists were wedded to Christian doctrine far more intimately than the 'occult' phase of interpretation discovers.

Furthermore, Hanegraaf, quoting Coudert on Alchemy, connects the practice to *Naturphilosophie* and esotericism, but questions whether 'spiritual' alchemy existed prior to the Renaissance[17].

Roger Bacon, writing in the thirteenth century, defined two forms of alchemy, the theoretical and the practical, both dealing in generation of products from the elements, but the latter more specifically which 'teaches how to make ... many other things better and more plentifully than they are made by nature'[18].

The Emerald Tablet

One of the basic texts of hermetic alchemy is "The Emerald Tablet" which can be seen as defining a number of the core concepts to the esoteric tradition; I have here quoted from Issac Newton's translation (c.1680), although many other versions of the translation are available;

1) Tis true without lying, certain & most true.
2) That wch is below is like that wch is above & that wch is above is like yt wch is below to do ye miracles of one only thing.
[...]
11a) So was ye world created.
12) From this are & do come admirable adaptaions whereof ye means (Or process) is here in this. [19]

This core alchemical text is fundamental to many esoteric doctrines, which in essence speak of:

1. A Correspondence between the Celestial and Terrestrial realms
2. A single origin
3. Unity in Diversity
4. Possibility of Transmutation

The Secret Beyond the Secret

Although the recently published and popularised "The Secret" references the Emerald Tablet, particularly in support of the idea of the "law of attraction", one can see that the Tablet holds many more fundamental truths, and is better read on its own merits, rather than through a post-modern new-age reading of its sublime secrets. The concept of mental frequencies and suchlike is not present in the Tablet's hermetic teachings, nor those of the Divine Pymander and other hermetic source-works. Similarly, the philosophical approach of 'creating' your own reality or 'alignment' is alien to the cosmology of the hermetic world-view.

I would recommend researching hermeticism and consulting the booklist of this course whilst reading references to the Emerald Tablet, and not reading it through interpretation! Similarly, the "secret" tends to promote an idea of "living as if" which is only semi-effective, according to sources on Magickal living; a ritual to effect change is always done as a "one-off", and then Universe is left to work without 'interference'. This requires faith, or as Aleister Crowley remarked, working "without lust of result".

This technique, for example used in Sigils, is the real secret of magickal living. Making the leap of faith is always guaranteed to produce effective results. However, obsessing about a desired aim is a guarantee of failure and is psychologically questionable.

Consider this - generally, we believe we have influence and control over our self and environment, to some extent. We often also believe in a Higher Power that has some cosmic scheme in mind, or at least that Universe has some direction or reasonable unfoldment, whose ultimate aim we cannot perceive.

But consider this further. Or indeed, even the opposite way around, as most magickal thinking appears the reverse of mundane notions - see the Hanged Man card of the Tarot. Consider that it is not that WE "create and do" and UNIVERSE "Wills & responds", but that UNIVERSE creates and WE Will. If you think about it, Universe has been happily creating for time immemorial. It's pretty good at it. But perhaps it is we who supply the direction. Imagine that.

The whole concept of manifesting a life at Will, so popular in new-age guides, is based on a fundamental illusion (one that is often referred to in the very same guides); that we are separate from something else. Without separation, there can be no control or concept of 'making things happen' i.e. I am separate to that in which things "happen". So it is more effective to reside in the truth and let Universe work. This is the silence of Harpocrates.

So a magickal life of alchemical transformation is created by observing natural change and learning from that change as happening in oneself; with no real division between "out there" and "inside"; suddenly other things start to happen, strange synchronicities occur, spontaneous changes take place.

Without any real effort. But the effort is in letting go of control and illusion, resting from the many distractions to attraction. Making an Alchemical Life is about shedding attachments, not going on a new-age binge of manifesting and accumulating more material in which one can support the illusion.

As Shakespeare had it,

> The weird sisters, hand in hand,
> Posters of the sea and land,
> Thus do go about, about:
> Thrice to thine and thrice to mine
> And thrice again, to make up nine.
> Peace! the charm's wound up.[20]

Shakespeare also returned to this knowledge of effective spell-casting in the Tempest, which is often less-quoted than Macbeth above;

> Sweet, now, silence!
> Juno and Ceres whisper seriously;
> There's something else to do: hush, and be mute,
> Or else our spell is marr'd.[21]

The role of Alchemy in the Western esoteric tradition

The **instrinsic** and **relative** components of esotericism according to Faivre[22] can be seen as recapitulations of the doctrine summarised by the Emerald Tablet, namely, Faivre's:

1. The idea of correspondences
2. Living Nature
3. Imagination and mediations
4. The experience of Transmutation

We can also see how Faivre's 'relative' components, "the praxis of concordance" and "transmission" are also exampled by alchemy in the esoteric tradition, lending significance to the work as the primary position or Asana of the tradition as a whole.

It could be argued that Alchemy is significant in the western tradition because it is an embodiment of the hermetic doctrine that defines the tradition itself, that hermetic doctrine providing synthesis and solvent of the multitude of philosophies comprising the canon of the tradition, be they neo-platonic, Aristotelian, or empirical post-renaissance science.

The History & Characters of Alchemy

Although there are many levels of alchemical work - Stanton J. Linden talks of pluralistic "alchemies" rather than the singular "alchemy"[23] and its practitioners are considered as "legion"[24]; from those "Masters of Fire" and "Divine Smiths"[25] to the ""Elect Sons of the Art"[26] - we will focus here primarily on the "Divine Halchymie"[27] and it's esoteric concerns. That is to say, alchemy discussed as having a correspondence with the state of the practitioner for its operation.

Alchemy has been variously treated as a "pretend science", discussed in common with such mass delusions as the Mississippi Scheme or Dutch Tulipomania[28] or a "flight from reason" in James Webb's titling, although he admits that:

> It is possible to imagine a moralising philosopher starting the whole business of speculative alchemy by finding in the laborious process of refining, combining and perfecting metal ore, an apt illustration of the way in which the soul must be purified, polished, and itself perfected to attain salvation.[29]

In an academic context, Faivre denotes three characteristics of the *pansophic* alchemy, particularly in the 17th century: 1) an interest in mythology as an allegorical system; 2) a partiality for elaborate illustrations; 3) the publication of encyclopaedic works and compendia.[30] It is these very elements that introduce the complexity of alchemical literature, using allegory and iconography in text and illustration to depict unknown processes in nature.

Current academic discourse remains developmental. In introducing the subject in the monumental and contemporary *Dictionary of Gnosis and Western Esotericism*, Lawrence M. Principe includes in his list of four "increasingly rejected" features, "the concept of alchemy as an essentially or primarily spiritual, psychic, or self-transformative endeavour" and talks of the "inherently unlikely character of this notion" - that is, Jung's view of alchemy being an 'irruption of the unconscious' which is 'projected' onto the contents of the flasks.[31]

However, such alchemists as Paracelsus "mainly regarded alchemy as important for the curing of disease and the prolongation of life"[32] rather than an entirely external discipline. Although Paracelsus indeed calls alchemy an art, with Vulcan its artist - denoting a more practical aspect - he also states that alchemy means;

> ... to carry to its end something that has not yet been completed.[33]

In this, alchemy is contextualised as having a cosmological and psychological application, in addition to the physical and medicinal formulation of the science.

Techne I: Alone I Work Higher Things.

Your First Alchemical Experiment - The Seed of Metals

In an alchemical document entitled The Stairway of the Wise, Escalier des Sages (1689), published in Groningen, Paris and Cologne, originally anonymously by the Flemish barent Coenders van Helpen, a series of engravings takes us through the elements and three main components of Alchemy; Sulpher, Mercury and Salt.

He gives a title for the engraving of Salt which is the Latin, Sal. He then gives SAL as the acronym for **S**olus **A**ltiora **L**aboro, 'Alone I work Higher Things'.

Materials: Salt, Bowl or Dish.

Experiment: Take the Salt and pour a reasonable amount, say four spoons, into the dish. Place the dish in a location by a window, where natural condensation may already be taking place. Otherwise place it in a kitchen or bathroom where water is present in the air.

Place the dish in the location, saying out loud, and firmly:

> AS THE SALT DRAWS FORTH, SO SHALL I OBSERVE,
> ALL THAT IS DRAWN OUT BEFORE MY EYES.

Leave the bowl and observe it over a period of at most 28 days, a full lunar cycle. You can start the experiment on a new or full moon if you already recognize these times in your work.

As the bowl starts to change, contemplate how the salt is being affected by the water which it is drawing to it. Notice how the water is being made visible by it becoming liquid from moisture vapor. What is the relationship between the salt and the water?

As your observations continue, notice and record any changes that occur in your environment that have a correspondence to your observations. It may be that something lost becomes found, something secret becomes known, or something avoided becomes actual. It may happen suddenly, or more likely over a period of time, as your observations continue.

This simple experiment establishes you in a unique position and mental *Asana* to Universe. You will start to perceive alchemy in an internal relationship to transformation that cannot be easily explained - and you should keep silent.

The maintaining of a hermetically sealed vessel is paramount to success. In this silence, the Alchemist creates pressure which appears to energize change. When you look at alchemical symbols, consider them silent, mute, only in that they are busy working. As the Sufi saying goes; the worker is hidden in the workshop.

When the twenty-eight day period is completed, you may wish to keep the contents of the bowl for use in the further technical workings of this course. Otherwise you may simply dispose of the contents by pouring them onto soil.

Praxis I

Your contemplation work will take you deep into the mysteries of Alchemy Imagery. In these meditations - or active visualisations - you will take the role of the Alchemist seeking Wisdom. You will go on six individual journeys which will continually deepen your experience of Alchemical principles.

To engage in these contemplations, it is suggested that you find a quiet place where you will be undisturbed for 20-45 minutes. Do not follow these visualisations for longer than one hour, as for a beginning student, this may result in slight disorientation or headaches for a while after the working.

You should arrange to eat and drink after following these workings to assist your grounding after spending time inwardly focusing. You may also use a bell or chime to commence and end the workings and suitable incense during the meditation. These will assist the transition between the outward and inward state and enhance the meditative experience. If you use music, ensure that it is reasonably quiet and neutral in tone. You may also choose music with an alchemical theme or structure, such as these chants:

http://www.predota.cz/index-en.html

For details of this music and its relationship to the Hermetic Alchemist, Michael Maier, see also:

http://www.radio.cz/en/article/88359

You should read the contemplation several times through in preparation, and perhaps make a few notes of key events and characters. You can also read these out loud and record them for playback whilst visualising. One simple method is to write down key navigation points (which are also summarised) on a large sheet of paper, so that by opening your eyes briefly at points during the working you can remind yourself where you should progress.

These six contemplations use key images in a famous series of sixty or so alchemical engravings from 1622. These are the J.D. Mylius's *Philosophia Reformata*, widely considered one of the masterpieces of alchemical engraving and directly influenced by the great hermetic philosophers Basil Valentine and Michael Maier.

The first month involves an additional - preparatory meditation, which should be carried out first, and then within two weeks the first formal praxis may be carried out. You may wish to repeat these meditations as your experience dictates. You should read them all through as a piece several times before you commence, but only read the detail of the particular working you are carrying out as you progress.

The meditations are as follows, and cover the first six stages of alchemy as given by a number of authors, including the Englishman George Ripley, in his *Compound of Alchemy* (1470):

- The Preparatory Praxis - *Elemental*
- The First Praxis - *Calcination*
- The Second Praxis - *Solution*
- The Third Praxis - *Separation*
- The Fourth Praxis - *Conjunction*
- The Fifth Praxis - *Putrefaction*
- The Sixth Praxis - *Congelation*

The illustrations for these stages have been taken from Mylius's *Philosophia Reformata* although that series uses a slightly extended version of the alchemical stages. It is important to realise that there is no singular agreed process by which the stone of the philosophers was created - indeed, there are many different opinions as to the nature of the stone itself.

The Preparatory Praxis - Establishing the Elements

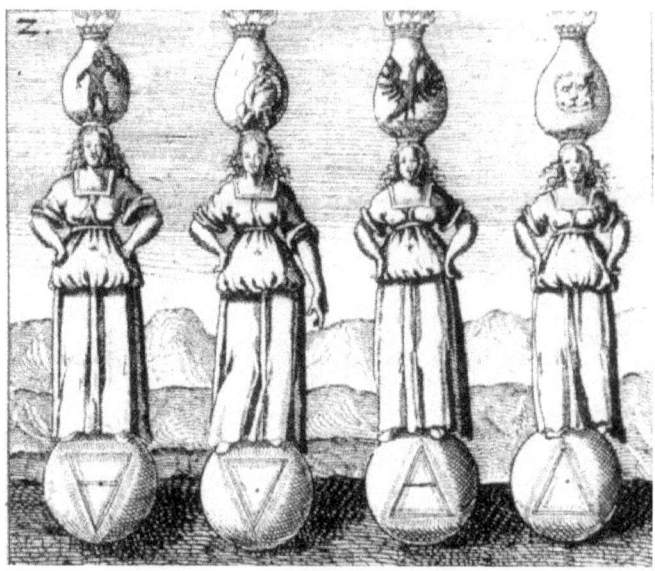

Creating an Alchemical Body

Close your eyes and visualise yourself dressed as an alchemist; imagine what you would wear to become an alchemist, working with the mysteries of nature, space and time. Perhaps you are robed like a magician, garbed as a chemist, dressed as an artist, or a worker of metals. Feel what it feels like to be dressed in this manner. Now visualise yourself creating another version of yourself, stood before you, facing ahead (so you can see this figures back). Imagine that as an alchemist you can create a slightly better image of yourself, perhaps only different in one slight detail, but making yourself a stronger image nonetheless. See how this figure stands, holds their head, moves slightly. When you are ready to take a deep breath, step forward and 'stand into' that new figure, immediately feeling what it feels like, seeing out through their eyes, hearing with their eyes.

Now look forwards in your imagination and create another figure - an even more transformed version of yourself, using your slightly improved skills as an alchemist. Perhaps this next version is even richer in detail, more confident, maybe they are even surrounded by flames or a shimmer of light. Make the image as powerful as you now can and when ready, taking a deep breath, step forward and inhabit that even more improved version, looking out through their eyes and feeling now all the abilities you possess. You may wish to repeat this at least three or four times.

Use sound, taste and smell whilst you strengthen your image; you may taste the clear taste of peppermint, or hear chimes, or smell rich incense that makes you think of gold. Use all your senses!

Entering the Alchemical Garden

When you are fully present in your transformed alchemical body you can visualise a portal in front of you with the word VITRIOL upon it:

This is often taken as an acronym for **V**isita **I**nteriora **T**errae **R**ectificando **I**nvenies **O**ccultum **L**apidem: 'Search the interior of the earth and by rectifying thou shalt find the hidden Stone'.

Step through this portal and find yourself in a beautifully ornate and designed garden, with neat hedges, rose-bushes, paths and trellises. This is the Alchemical Garden and will be your meeting-place in vision and dream with the alchemical archetypes. Wander through the garden noting any details; perhaps there are statues, fountains, streams and bridges.

At last come to a central area, a cobbled square, perhaps, or other square space. Some people find themselves on a lawn, or an enclosed part of a hedge-maze.

Establishing the Elements

On each side of the square, you will see a female figure holding a jar, perhaps as illustrated for this working. Each of the figures is robed and the robe bears the symbol of the element for which the person is an avatar; Air, Fire, Water and Earth. You can use the traditional symbols as illustrated, or you may see simple icons such as a mountain for Earth, a flame for Fire, a wave for Water, and a cloud for Air.

Approach the figure of Air, in the eastern side of the square. Ask her if you may ask a question of Alchemical Art. When she has assented, ask her:

- What is in the Jar of Air and how does it serve me?

Take the answer from the figure, who may also show you what is in the jar, for example, a bird in the jar of Air, as the original illustration. This answer may also be given as a cryptic message, a symbol, a sign, or a riddle. It may be simple. Say it out loud so that you can recall it, and thank the figure for her time. You may also ask, if you wish:

- How may I honour the element of Air more in my alchemical life?

Then approach the figure of Fire, and ask the same question(s), and when you have thanked the figure, do likewise with the figures of Water and Earth.

When you have received your answers from the four elemental figures, you may return to the portal by which you entered the garden (you may find this will move sometimes, do not be concerned about this) and step through it. As you do so, take a deep breath, and open your eyes to return to full consciousness, bringing with you all the positive experiences and learnings.

Some further ideas that may help you make the most of this praxis:

- Make a note of your experience straight away.
- Write down any quotes given to you.
- Make notes of any feelings you had at any point in the praxis.
- Draw sketches if you wish of the garden or the figures.
- Note any symbols that you may need to research.

You should now get grounded by eating or drinking, and return to your notes later. You may notice powerful dreams as you start to activate the alchemical archetypes, so make sure you have a dream journal by your bed and record any dreams as you progress through the six-month working.

The occultist Aleister Crowley noted that the Alchemical Plane was very distinct, and in time you will find it has a certain quality to it that differs from other types of pathworking, scrying or visualisation. It is truly unique in content and atmosphere. I describe it as "baroque"; it can feel 'cold' compared to, for example, a shamanic voyage, but it has a hidden heat to it that you will discover.

Navigation Points

1. Create an Alchemical Body
2. Go through a Portal marked VITRIOL
3. Enter a Garden
4. Find a Square
5. Meet the Four Elements; Air (E), Fire (S), Water (W) and Earth (N)
6. Ask each what is in their jar and how it serves you?
7. Ask each how you may honour their element?
8. Thank all figures
9. Return

The First Praxis - Calcination

As Ripley puts it in his verse for the process of *calcination*, which he considers the first stage of Alchemy;

> Calcination is the purgation of our stone,
> And restoration also of its natural heat[34]

The process of calcination is a gradual heating of a material until it is reduced to ashes or can easily be powdered. The heating is carried out below the boiling point of the material, over a long period of time. In terms of magickal alchemy, this signifies the work of exhaustion that comes from the student trying many different routes of enquiry. Over time, one comes to question everything about life, Universe and Self. This inevitably leads to a weakening of old ideas and habitual forms of perception, breaking down beliefs until the original self is revealed. This is calcination, and requires a gradual heat over a long period of time to accomplish a comprehensive purging rather than a complete break-down! It restores, as Ripley says, a natural energy to the Initiate, coming from living a life true to the self, not out-moded beliefs and values, which are reduced to "powder" ready for the next stage, *solution*.

In psychological terms, the process of calcination is likened to the initial drying-out of a person's complexes, desires and confusions in the 'fire' of psychotherapy. The behaviours which result in shame, guilt and anxiety are brought out to dry in order to separate them from the unconscious desires in which they are soaked.[35]

The Furnace of the Alchemist

Enter into your Alchemical body as before. Enter the portal of Vitriol and proceed to the Square of the Elements. Now ask the figure of Fire to direct you to the Furnace of the Alchemist. Follow her directions until you approach a building in which you will see a room from which emerges a great but dry heat, such as that provided by a sauna.

Entering into that room you will see a table at which sit three figures; the Moon, the Sun, and the Winged Guide, as you will see in the illustration.

Approach the three figures, and ask the Guide:

- What is the matter that I must subject to calcination?

You may receive an answer from the Guide, the Moon figure or the Sun figure, or all three. Say the answer out loud so that you may recall it easier when you have completed the praxis. If you receive an object from the figures, you may place this into the furnace. It may be that on future occasions, you will bring certain objects to place into the furnace as your understanding widens of this work of calcination.

Another general question to ask at any stage of Inner Workings is:

- How in my outer life may I develop the energy that is present here?

For example, you could ask how you should act or behave to promote the calcination of old habits, or if there is a new activity you can do to engage with the process of solution. You can ask if there are new perspectives or beliefs you should consider, or pay attention to, in order to honour the energy which is represented by a figure in your praxis, for example asking, "How may I honour the Lion?" The advantage of working this way is that it allows your own route of discovery within the realm of these powerful archetypes.

If you wish to make further enquiries, you may ask the Guide figure;

- What are the Ashes of Herme's Tree and how may they be used?

This will allow you to explore some of the mysteries of Alchemy as given by Ripley. You might also approach the lion, which is eating a serpent, and contemplate what this might mean, again, by seeing assistance from the Guide.

Once you have completed your enquiries and experiments in the place of the Furnace of the Alchemist, you may return to the Square of the Elements and leave through the Portal of Vitriol. Re-orientate yourself as previously, ensuring that you drink plenty of water having worked in the dry heat.

Navigation Points

1. Make your way to the Square of the Elements as before.
2. Seek direction from the figure of Fire to the Furnace of the Alchemist
3. Enter the furnace-room
4. Meet with the Sun, Moon and Guide figure
5. Ask the Guide what it is that you must give to calcination
6. Place any objects given to you into the furnace
7. Ask if there is anything else you need to do to promote your calcination
8. Thank all figures
9. Return

Now, you may also wonder that you are indeed through the first gate of the alchemical castle, which has twelve gates, and that you will travel five more before this present praxis is complete:

> You are now within the first gate,
> Of the Castle where the Philosophers dwell.
> Proceed wisely that you may win,
> And go though more gates of that Castle.
> This Castle is round as any bell,
> And gates it has yet eleven more,
> One is conquered, now to the second go[36]

Reading 1c (Source Material): The Invisible Mountain

The source material readings are your opportunity to read original alchemical texts, with the context of this course to guide your understanding. It is hoped you will see further detail in each reading of these source materials as you progress through the exercises of this course. The materials have been chosen to be relevant to each module, and provide a wealth of further material for your study. Where extracts are made, it is suggested if you find inspiration in the material, you consult the reading list for the full text source.

Our first extract is a short allegorical story from a collection of alchemical texts, *Lumen de Lumine, or A New Magical Light Discovered and Communicated to the World*, (London, 1651) by Thomas Vaughan (1622-1666). It clearly depicts in symbolic form the spiritual aspects required to discover the *mountain at midnight*, and furthermore alludes to the presence of a Guide who is not known to the alchemist but is indispensable.

Extract from Lumen de Lumine (1651)

There is a mountain situated in the midst of the earth, or center of the world, which is both small and great. It is soft, also above measure hard and stony. It is far off, and near at hand, but by the providence of God, invisible. In it are hidden most ample treasures, which the world is not able to value. This mountain by envy of the devil, who always opposeth the glory of God and the happiness of man, is compassed about with very cruel beasts and other [sic] ravenous birds, which make the way thither both difficult and dangerous; and therefore hitherto, because the time is not yet come, the way thither could not be sought after nor found out. But now at last the way is to be found by those that are worthy, but notwithstanding by every man's self-labor and endeavors.

To this mountain you shall go in a certain night (when it comes) most long and most dark, and see that you prepare yourselves by prayer. Insist upon the way that leads to the mountain, but ask not of any man where the way lies: only follow your Guide, who will offer himself to you, and will meet you in the way but you shall not know him. This Guide will bring you to the mountain at midnight, when all things are silent and dark. It is necessary that you arm yourselves with a resolute heroic courage, lest you fear those things that will happen, and so fall back. You need no sword, nor any other bodily weapons, only call upon God sincerely and heartily.

When you have discovered the mountain, the first miracle that will appear is this. A most vehement and very great wind, that will shake the mountain and shatter the rocks to pieces. You shall be encountered also by lions and dragons and other terrible beasts, but fear not any of these things. Be resolute and rake heed that you return not, for your Guide who brought you thither will not suffer any evil to befall you. As for the treasure, it is not yet discovered but it is very near. After this wind will come an earthquake, that will overthrow those things which the wind hath left and make all flat. But be sure that you fall not off.

The earthquake being past, there shall follow a fire, that will consume the earthly rubbish, and discover the treasure, but as yet you cannot see it. After all these things and near the daybreak there shall be a great calm, and you shall see the Day-Star arise and the dawning will appear, and you shall perceive a great treasure. The chiefest thing in it, and the most perfect, is a certain exalted tincture, with which the world (if it served God and were worthy of such gifts) might be tinged and turned into most pure gold.

This tincture being used, as your Guide shall reach you, will make you young when you are old, and you shall perceive no disease in any part of your bodies. By means of this tincture also you shall find pearls of that excellency which cannot be imagined. But do not you arrogate anything to yourselves because of your present power, but be contented with that which your Guide shall communicate to you. Praise God perpetually for this His gift, and have a special care that you use it not for worldly pride, but employ it in such works which are contrary to the world. Use it rightly and enjoy it so, as if you had it not. Live a temperate life, and beware of all sin, otherwise your Guide will forsake you, and you shall be deprived of this happiness. For know this of a truth, whosoever abuseth this tincture and lives not exemplarly, purely, and devoutly before men he shall lose this benefit, and scarce any hope will there be left ever to recover it afterwards.

Theoria I: Alchemy and Hermeticism

Your First Homework Assignment - The Emerald Tablet

As we have already seen, the text known as the Emerald Tablet is a primary source for not only Alchemy, but much of what became known as *hermeticism*; teaching said to be derived from the threefold Hermes, *Hermes Trismigestus*. Holmyard, Davis and others all consider that this Tablet may be one of the earliest of all alchemical works.

It should be remarked that the Greeks and Egyptians used the term translated as 'emerald' for emeralds, green granites, and perhaps green jasper. The oldest known source for the text of the Emerald Tablet is the *Kitab Sirr al-Asrar*, a compendium of advice for rulers authored by Abd al-Qadir al-Jilani in around 800 AD. This work was translated into Latin as *Secretum Secretorum* (The Secret of Secrets) by Johannes "Hispalensis" or Hispaniensis (John of Seville) ca. 1140 and by Philip of Tripoli c. 1243.

The Latin Text and Contemporary Translation can be found here:

http://en.wikipedia.org/wiki/Emerald_Tablet

The Theoria work of this first module is for you to study the text of the Emerald Tablet and begin writing a commentary on its enigmatic verses. Collect quotes for each line which relates to the idea expressed by the line, events and even pictures that assist you to observe the cosmology implied by the tablet in your everyday life. You might, for example, be at a recycling plant, and see various operations being carried out which manifest the ideas of the tablet.

The Emerald Tablet of Hermes Tristmegistus

It is true without untruth, certain and most true:

that which is below is like that which is on high, and that which is on high is like that which is below; by these things are made the miracles of one thing.

And as all things are, and come from One, by the mediation of One, So all things are born from this unique thing by adaption.

The Sun is the father and the Moon the mother.

The wind carries it in its stomach. The earth is its nourisher and its receptacle.

The Father of all the *Theleme* of the universal world is here.

Its force, or power, remains entire,
if it is converted into earth.

You separate the earth from the fire, the subtle from the gross, gently with great industry.

It climbs from the earth and descends from the sky, and receives the force of things superior and things inferior.

You will have by this way, the glory of the world and all obscurity will flee from you.

It is the power strong with all power, for it will defeat every subtle thing and penetrate every solid thing
In this way the world was created.

From it are born wonderful adaptations, of which the way here is given.

That is why I have been called *Hermes Tristmegistus*, having the three parts of the universal philosophy.

This, that I have called the solar Work, is complete.

[Translated from Fulcanelli 1964: 312.]

http://www.levity.com/alchemy/emerald.html

Module 2: Solution

The process of Solution is appropriate for our second module. It is also the second stage in Ripley's version of the alchemical stages, of which he had twelve in total. Our introductory course therefore takes us half-way through the twelve gates. At our second stage, and the second stage of any creative process, we find that our original ideas have become loosened by our actual practice and events. It is a time when our plan may be overturned and our resolve weakened. The stage of Solution is perhaps best depicted by the Tarot card of the Moon.

However, we must accept this dissolving of fixed assumptions, and reflect upon the changes we must make, to move forwards. In time we will welcome change as essential to all transformation, and as an indication of progress, not as an obstacle. Here we learn such alchemical attitudes to life.

Reading 2a (General): Alchemy and the Manufacture of Revelation

The emblematic language of Alchemy, referred to as the Western Mandala by Adam Mclean, holds a significant place in the esoteric tradition.[37] As the tracing boards in Masonic ritual demonstrate 'teaching stories' (a classic example is Cagliostro's eight Masonic watercolours executed by de Loutherbourg in 1786)[38] so do the alchemical illustrations.

According to Obrist (2003), the "verbal and pictorial similes in alchemical documents may be divided into two main groups: analogies, on the one hand, and diverse rhetorical forms of figurative speech – allegory, metaphor, enigma – on the other."[39]

We intuitively recognise Alchemical diagrams, indeed as Crowley stated, "There is a unique quality about the Alchemical Plane which renders its images instantly recognisable,"[40] those images being, to one 'Rising on the Planes,'[41] "those of gardens curiously kept, mountains furnished with peculiar symbols, hieroglyphic animals, and pictures like the 'Goldseekers' and the 'Massacre of the Innocents' of Basil Valentine."[42] It is this same recognition which is activated in the *praxis* work of this course.

The world of Alchemy is presented as a paradisiacal world, in which corruption is played out. The motif of the garden is utilised, as well as pagan animal imagery, which alchemy blends as a meta-mythological structure, perhaps even a trans-mythical construct. In this, alchemy will always remain significant in the esoteric tradition as providing an illustrative language of mystical transformation. It answers Faivre's characteristic of 'transmission' in providing a means of passing on teaching that requires an 'initiated' perspective to be understood, which initiation can only be provided by one already initiated, or by grace, or by performing the work itself, which unfolds its mysteries to the deserving. In this alchemy is a *self-extracting program*, both practically and mystically.

Additionally, the language of alchemy is transformative in itself; the symbols and illustrations were designed as meditative artefacts, to engender the state being illustrated. In this they intended to manufacture revelation, not merely illustrate it.

Techne II: Basic Principles of Growth and Transformation

Your Second Alchemical Experiment: The Power of Salt

A certain thing is found in this world,
Which is also everywhere, and in every place,
It is not earth, nor fire, nor air, nor water,
However it wants neither of these things,
Nay, it can become fire, air, water, and earth;
For it contains all nature, in itself purely, and sincerely,
It becomes white and red, is hot and cold,
It is moist and dry, and is diversifiable every way,
The band of sages only have known it,
And they call it their salt.

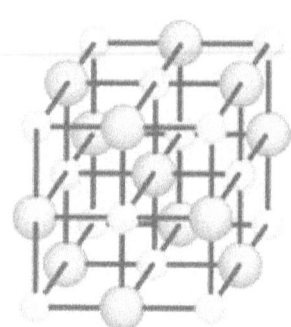

In this second experiment we will work again with salt. This time, rather than being a passive material, we will grow our own crystals and see salt as a generative principle. As you prepare this experiment, contemplate that you are about to create order out of chaos. For the alchemist, this is an important principle; all work seeks to observe order in nature.

Whilst the crystals grow, you may wish to sketch the results, or produce artwork inspired by the patterns which you will observe. Many alchemical illustrations contain patterns and shapes inspired by the observation of transformative processes. As you progress, you will see more patterns in alchemical icons and respond to them naturally through your own experience.

Materials

- 1/4 cup table salt
- 2 teaspoons vinegar
- 1 cup water
- Shallow dish, jar lid, or container
- Storage container
- Sponge
- Scissors

Experiment

1. Cut a sponge so it fits in the bottom of the dish, container, or lid. Put the sponge in the bottom of the dish.

2. Boil water. Remove from heat, and add a generous 1/4 cup of salt a little at a time. Stir well after each addition of salt.

3. Add vinegar. Stir well.

4. Pour the salt and vinegar mixture carefully over the sponge, just enough to cover the bottom of the dish. Pour the extra mixture into a container and save.

5. Put the dish in a safe, sunny place. After a few days, salt crystals will start to form. If the salt and vinegar mixture evaporates, add more.

You will see that cubic salt crystals form, and as time passes, these will grow.

As they do so, observe in your outer life how you experience people and events; attempt to discern how they are generated from first principles, and how the world of action (*Assiah* in Kabbalah) unfolds in the way as the salt crystals. Notice how structure is inherent, yet not always visible. Notice how one shape has many variations.

You may wonder how life and crystals are related; if crystals can grow, what is life and creation? Contemplate again the Emerald Tablet for further inspiration as to what you are actually witnessing in this simple experiment.

When you are satisfied that you have grown several crystals, retain these for use in the later *techne* work and dispose of the remaining materials.

Reading 2b (Source material): The Stages of the Work

The source material chosen for the second module deals with the stages of the alchemical process. Here we read Stephan Michelspacher in *Cabala, Spiegel der Kunst und Natur in Alchymia*, published in 1615. We see here a combination of systems used to illustrate the path of the alchemist; elemental, planetary, and zodiacal. We also see here the Christian approach to alchemy, trusting in God alone. However, notice that there are two alchemists in the illustration; one is blind to the mountain and the steps, the other is following Nature, into the earth. This reminds us of our portal in the praxis, called Vitriol.

In this brief extract, note the implicit explaination of a doctrine of eternal life, which is promised to those ascending the alchemical stairway. Also examine the text for alchemical, hermetic, kabbalistic and Christian doctrine, which here find a synthesis.

Extract from The Portal of the Amphitheatre (1615)

This is the Portal of the amphitheatre of the only true and eternal Wisdom--a narrow one, indeed, but sufficiently august, and consecrated to Jehovah. To this portal ascent is made by a mystic, indisputably prologetic, flight of steps, set before it as shown in the picture. It consists of seven theosophic, or, rather, philosophic steps of the Doctrine of the Faithful Sons. After ascending the steps, the path is along the way of God the Father, either directly by inspiration or by various mediate means. According to the seven oracular laws shining at the portal, those who are inspired divinely have the power to enter and with the eyes of the body and of the mind, of seeing, contemplating and investigating in a Christiano-Kabalistic, divino-magical, physico-chemical manner, the nature of the Wisdom: Goodness, and Power of the Creator; to the end that they die not sophistically but live theosophically, and that the orthodox philosophers so created may with sincere philosophy expound the works of the Lord, and worthily praise God who has thus blessed these friends of God.

Praxis II

The Second Praxis - Solution

Solution immediately follows the calcination, and involves the element of water, applied to the results of the fire of the first process. However, like most alchemical process, it is actually a combination of elements. Thus, in performing solution, a hidden fire is revealed. This is depicted in the illustration by both the male figure surrounded by flames, and the lion disgorging the sun.

In psychological and magical-initiatory terms, the process of Solution is that related to the Moon Tarot card - a bitter time of self-discovery, as one's own beliefs, now exposed by the calcination of self-examination, are found to be nothing more than automatic patterns of a self-serving ego. The more one contemplates and analyses (Mercury) oneself, the worse it seems to get. Eventually, it feels like the entire self has been dissolved, and there is nothing left but an empty core. On the outside, it is a fire which burns away everything, but on the inside it is water which dissolves all that we used to be.[43] This process is perilous, and requires great integrity and often a teacher, someone who has already gone through this stage.[44]

Discovering the White Water

Enter into your Alchemical body and make your way through the Portal of Vitriol into the Square of the Elements. You may notice at various times of working this praxis that the time of day changes in the Alchemical Garden, or even the Season. You should note these changes in your magical journal if you keep one, which is recommended and useful as you progress.

You will approach the figure of Water and ask her to direct you to the Place of White Water. Follow her directions, until you come to a location where you find a large container which is sealed shut, as you will see in the diagram. Do not be concerned if your visualisation provides you a different type of container, or size, so long as it is sealed shut and is where you have been directed by the figure of Water. If you do not find the location or container immediately, return to the Square and ask directions again - you may have to accomplish some other activity before you can find the White Water. This could be in the Inner or Outer World. Sometimes, you may be given an instruction to wait a certain period of time, for example, having to return in three days. You should trust these instructions even if they appear cryptic.

In all these workings, you should also go to the Winged Guide if you need further clarification or confirmation, but most importantly, trust your instinct and common-sense. Do not follow any instructions that you would otherwise not action, unless you are comfortable. Of course, you must not follow any directions that contravene usual accepted behaviour - treat your Inner World as another source of deep insight and inspiration but remain in charge of your Will and Action at all times throughout such workings.

Invoking the Alchemical Venus

Once you have found the container of White Water - which is an alchemical name for Mercury - ask aloud for the figure of Venus to be present with you. You can use your own words, or use this version, based on various alchemical works:

> Fair Sister, come unto me,
> Immaculate Dove, descend
> Lady of Love may I now see,
> Hither come as my friend.

When you have called upon Venus, and a figure has arrived in your place of working, you must ask her the following:

- How may I release the hidden fire through solution?

At this point, the Lion may appear as may an image of the sun, or some other fire. Take the advice given to you by the lady Venus, and observe the Lion or the Sun. You should start to feel an internal warmth arise that may cause your skin to tingle. Recall the figure in the first illustration that was yourself - the alchemist. In this second praxis, you are taking the place of the 'man of Flame' which you can see in the illustration. The work of Solution, although carried out by water, releases a hidden fire.

You may also wish to link the processes together in further workings by taking an object from the Winged Guide, placing it in the Furnace until it is reduced to ashes. You then remove the ashes and bring them to the place of White Water, where you dissolve the ashes by pouring the contents of the container - the Mercurial white water - onto the ashes. You may find something transforms, or grows, out of the work. You may ask the figure of Venus what you must now do with this issue.

When you have received your answer, worked with the white water, or made any other experiments you wish to make in this place, you may thank the figures and return.

A Great Secret of Calcination and Solution

Ripley also states the following, which to the un-initiated may sound cryptic, but if you have followed the two basic practices above you will begin to understand:

> And here a secret I will disclose to you,
> Which is the ground unto our secrets all,
> Which if you do not know you shall but lose,
> Thy labour and costs both great and small.
> Take heed therefore that in error you not fall,
> **The more your earth, and the less your water be,**
> **The rather and better solution shall you see**.

That is to say, the more you have done with your calcination, the more ashes you will have made, the less solution you will have to go through, and the easier it will be to attain a complete result. As one alchemist wrote; tire not of calcination.

Reading 2c (Academic): Dream Alchemy

Jung's attempts to actually interpret alchemical texts as dreams, containing archetypal imagery, is frustrated in part by the lack of definition of the symbolism in the cultural environment of the alchemists, and their lack of conformity in utilising the symbolism.

Although Jung worked on the *Mysterium Coniunctionis*, the Eirenaus philalethes, *Introitus apertus...*, Michael Maier's *Symbola aureae mensae,* and Abraham Eleazar's *Uraltes Chymisches Werck* he writes:

> In order to interpret dreams we need some knowledge of the dreamer's personal situation, and to understand alchemical parables we must know something about the symbolic assumptions of the alchemists. We amplify dreams by the personal history of the patient and the parables by the statements found in the text.[45]

James Hillman writes that alchemy:

> incorporate[s] events that one can touch and see. The work of soul-making requires corrosive acids, heavy earths, ascending birds; there are sweating kings, dogs and bitches, stenches, urine and blood. How like the language of our dreams and how unlike the language into which we interpret dreams[46]

The interface between dream, waking and vision is often alluded to in alchemical writings. Here we quote the 15th Century French alchemical allegory of John of the Fountain:

> Then after eating I fell asleep within this pleasant orchard. And according to my apprehension, I slept long enough for the pleasure which I took, being in the dream which I dreamed. You now may know it from my dream, and I after found it a fiction.[47]

The ability to utilise Alchemical iconography as a meditation is carefully described in the sixteenth century *Le Tableau des Riches Inventions*:

> That if during the time of this blessed rest one enters into some difficult visions, & that the soul should be forced by unhappy apprehensions, one may easily withdraw, if by shaking loose this bad spot, one reintegrates oneself in the goodness of one's quietest respite: & if it should also happen, (as is most common as nature inclines to all contentment) the spirit is softly wrapped in the agreeable shades of the opportune sweetness of prosperous fantasies which conveniently relieve the heart, one diverts oneself, one dives therein, & dwelling prettily therein, one remains in this ease as long as one can, in order to savor at length the delicious pleasure which is perceived in such felicity.[48]

François Béroalde de Verville (1556-1626) defined this *steganography* as 'the art of representing plainly that which is easily conceived but which under the coarsened features of its appearance hides subjects quite other than that which seems to be represented...'

As a case example of how alchemical iconography was interpreted in a purely psychoanalytic framework, we will look briefly at the *Rosarium Philosophorum*, an alchemical work from the 16th Century, which was extensively utilised by Jung.

The Rosarium

The first printed edition of the *Rosarium philosophorum* was published in *De alchimia opuscula complura veterum philosophorum*, vol. II, Frankfurt 1550[49]. It consists of some twenty illustrations of a sequence in which two figures - a King and Queen - are subjected to various transformations (in the most part, within a bath) although other symbolism is present, including a Lion devouring the Sun, a Resurrected Figure and a Fountain.

Illustrations: Images 4, 18, 20 from the *Rosarium philosophorum* (1550)

Jung referred to the *Rosarium* as the "most complete and simplest illustration" of the importance of the *hierosgamos* in the alchemical process, and he furthermore compared their symbolism to the phenomenon of *transference*.[50]

He particularly engaged the iconography of the divine pair and the water of life as indicating the individuation process taking place between the *anima* and *animus* in the unconscious, although he often extended the symbols to other tasks, such as comparing the imagery of the death of the sun to the descent of the Gnostic *Nous* (mind) into *Physis* (physical nature).[51]

He furthermore commented that the "alchemist, too, dreams in his own specific language," and that as the *Rosarium* states, "only he who knows the secret of the stone understands their words".[52]

The *Rosarium Philosophorum* (Frankfurt, 1550) has also been studied academically for its wealth of symbolism and its depiction of the alchemical process - Karen-Claire Voss concludes;

> It is not surprising that the author of the *Rosarium Philosophorum* chose images of the *hierosgamos* to help convey something of the exquisitely subtle reciprocity invoked in the alchemical *coniunctio*. The *hierosgamos* images of alchemy are profoundly eloquent expressions of the experience of the true adepts as they moved through the later stages of the work. For those alchemists, *all* the elements of ordinary experience were sacralised.[53]

Theoria II: Alchemy, the Individual and Universe

Alchemy as a Humanist Technology

In essence, Alchemy is a humanist technology; "the beliefs of humanism are not based on revelation in the supernatural sense, but on the revelations that science and learning have given us about man and the universe. A humanist believes with full assurance that man is not alien to nature, but a part of nature, albeit a unique one. He is made of the same matter and works by the same energy as the rest of the universe."

"As regards the individual, a humanist religion will, like the ancient Greeks, stress excellence. But as complementary to this, it will go further than the Greek principle of moderation: nothing too much -- and will make psychological integration and total wholeness an essential aim, and in some sense the equivalent of the state of salvation in Christian terminology."[54]

Alchemy, since inception, has maintained a polyphasic model which has led to inevitable confusion when approached through a modern monophasic viewpoint. In effect, Alchemy has always stated that we are changed by the work – in this it is a very modern outlook shared with the new Alchemy of Quantum Physics. Indeed, looking at the cover of New Scientist (3rd July 2004) whose cover depicts a mandala-like diagram, and the cover for Eliade's "Forge and Crucible" on the origins and structures of Alchemy, one would presume they were dealing with identical subjects. In fact, the cover headings on the New Scientist magazine are "Pentaquark: A riddle at the root of reality," and "The Immortality Factor" which indicates there is indeed little new under the sun.

Heisenberg's Uncertainty Principle, Schrondingers Cat, Lilly's human bio-computer model, Sarfatti's Participator meta-principle[55], all point to the holographic model of consciousness that Alchemy assumed from first principles.

Alchemy and the Unfinished Universe

Parcelsus wrote that "Alchemy [is] perfecting what Nature had left in an imperfect state," and in this context it is a precursor to the evolutionary views of Teilhard de Chardin and scientific writers such as Louise B. Young, author of *The Unfinished Universe*[56].

In The New Chemical Light (Sendivogius), the dialogue between the Alchemist and Mercury is interjected upon by Nature herself, who chastises the ignorance of the alchemist and of those who truly perform the work, she says,

Nature: ... they clear away the impediments that I may sooner reach my goal.

This fundamental position was stated as early as 300 C.E. when Zosimos, an Egyptian alchemist, conversant with both the works of Hermes Trismegistus and the Greek corpus hermeticum stated his view of alchemy "as providing the means by which nature itself can pass from an imperfect state to a regenerate one."[57]

As theurgy concerned itself originally with the animation of inert matter by means of telestike (ritual), alchemy sought to perfect inert matter, which leads us to the role Alchemy bears upon the initiatory systems of the esoteric tradition.

It could be argued that quantum physics and cosmology, specifically String Theory and the quest for a 'Theory of Everything' is a continuation of the alchemical quest, and as such is a significant bridge between the mystical concerns of the esoteric student and those of the scientific world. Indeed, the latest theoretical underpinnings of M-theory could be aligned with the alchemical or kabbalistic cosmologies with little effort[58]; one model of M-theory utilises 10 dimensions, 4 of space and time, and 6 'rolled-up' dimensions, as indicated similarly by the Kabbalistic glyph, the Tree of Life.

Your Theoria work for this second module is to question in what way alchemy was a pre-cursor for modern chemistry, and how do the theories of quantum physics and fluid dynamic theories also provide reflections on alchemical concerns?

Module 3: Separation

In Separation, the material of the alchemist, having already been through calcination and solution, begins to separate out. Fixed ideas have been broken through, and dissolved by analysis and experience. It is a strange time when nothing feels fixed, and the mind is full of apparently separate ideas and perspectives. It is hard to pin any one thing down, and ideas constantly move about, like oil on water. The alchemist here has to learn that this separation is again, only a part of a longer work.

Patience is the virtue he must here exercise, in order to continue his progress. It may also seem that he enters a waking sleep, or his awareness starts to fragment into different states at different times. If he is learning, this is a difficult and frustrating time, when he doubts that he will ever see the big picture.

As with all stages of alchemy, it is possible to give up, admit failure, a moment before the result is gained.

Reading 3a (Academic): The Alchemical Amphitheatre

Khunrath and the Amphitheatre

The 1608 frontispiece of *Amphitheatrum Sapientiae Aeternae* clearly demonstrates that 'Christiano-Kabalisticum, Divino-Magicum, and Physico-Chymicum' were to Khunrath the key elements of the eternal wisdom[59].

Khunrath (1560 – 1605), who derived the central theme of *Amphitheatrum* from the magical book *Arbatel*, i.e. theosophia as a meta-science[60], denoted the true sciences as including **Physica**, **Mageia** and **Cabala**, which he defined thus in his 'Annotationes' to the *Amphitheatrum* [61]:

Physica consists of the knowledge and examination of both the great world as a whole as well as the little world. Knowledge ensues from tradition, nature and art and can be won out of the scripture, the Philosopher's Stone, and ourselves.

Mageia is called the wisdom of the most ancient sages of various nations and consists in the cult of divine beings in the communion and conversation with spirits. Its achievements are the same as the perfect study of the Kabbalah amongst the Hebrews, although the latter, guided by a gracious hand, have progressed much further in this field.

Cabala is the theosophical reception of divine revelation, through which man may know both God and his Messiah as well as the pure forms, the nature of the great and little world, and also himself; because this Kabbalah reveals to man the true sense of the Holy Scripture and at the same time enables him to unite with God and the higher intelligences and to rejoice in them.

The *Arbatel* gives the following definition of Magic, which can be seen as a predecessor to Khunrath's viewpoint:

> '*Magia est connexio a viro sapiente agentium per naturam cum patientibus, sibi, congruenter respondentibus, ut inde opera prodeant, non sine corum admiratione qui causam ignorant.*
>
> Magick is the connexion of natural agents and patients, answerable each to other, wrought by a wise man, to the bringing forth of such effects as are wonderful to those that know not their causes.'[62]

Referring to Hermes Trismegistus, Khunrath continues that the true sciences can only be acquired at the 'University of God', and 'through theosophical mental practice and divine inspiration in the oratory and through constant personal labour in the laboratory'[63]

Johann Arndt (1555-1621), a Lutheran theologian and friend of Khunrath's, wrote 'Where Magia ends, Cabala begins, where Cabala ends, Theologia and the prophetic spirit begins.'[64] In this we see at this historical stage, the synthesis of the three traditions was weighted towards Theosophy, with Magic and Cabala as forerunners. We also see in the writings of the magician, Eliphas Levi, that this weighting was later reversed, setting the stage for the flourishing of 'western magic' in the 19th century.

Techne III: Creating a Nexus

Your Third Alchemical Experiment: The Seed of Salt

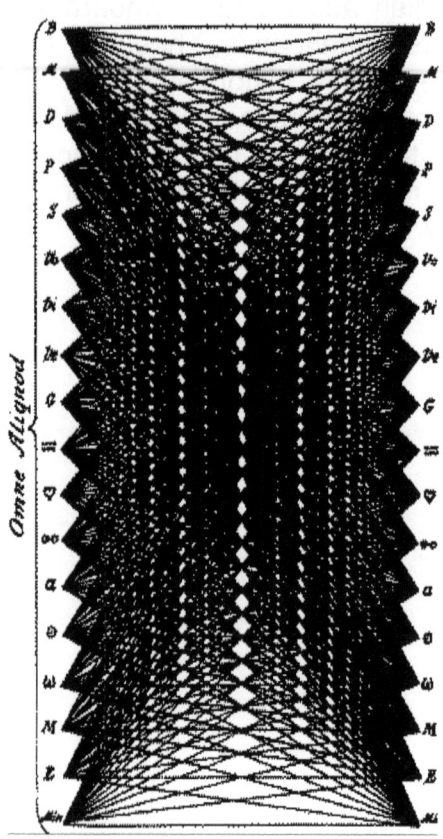

In our third working in the Path of Salt, we will see how the Salt that we have used both as a passive agent of *invocation* (calling forth water from the air) and an active agent of *evocation* (evoking developmental growth of crystals) can also be used as an agent of *summoning*. For those that work with ritual magick or grimoire magick, you may see in this paragraph a great secret as to the usage of alchemy within ritual which goes beyond this present course.

To summon or attract by salt, we view the salt crystal itself as a seed, or a nexus point, known in Chaos Physics as a 'strange attractor'. This is a mathematical concept which goes towards explaining how certain formulae appear to gravitate towards a solution, or their graphical representations form islands of order in apparent chaos, such as Fractals. The book, *Chaos,* by James Gleik is a good reference for these concepts.

Materials

- A good-sized crystal grown from previous praxis
- A length of nylon or fishing-line
- A small length of dowel rod sufficient to go across the jar mouth
- A jar
- Salt
- Water

Optional: Mesh to cover jar (prevents dust settling into water) with small hole in centre through which the line can be passed.

Experiment

Fasten the small seed crystal to one end of the nylon line by tying a simple knot around the crystal. Cotton or other material is not suitable as crystals may grow on the material. For one experiment I simply used a length of protected line from a garden 'strimmer'.

Measure the length of the line sufficient to suspend the crystal about mid-way in the jar, and tie off the other end to the dowel rod. This will then be placed across the mouth of the jar to suspend the crystal mid-way.

Boil sufficient water to three-quarter fill the jar.

Stir salt into the boiled water in medium amounts until it is full saturated (i.e. no more salt can dissolve into the water). This is also known as a brine solution.

Allow the water to cool sufficiently to pour it into the jar.

Suspend the seed salt crystal in the solution.

You may place a mesh over the mouth of the jar, with a small hole through which the nylon can pass, which will protect the solution from dust.

Place the jar gently in a position where it can attract sunlight but is not subject to many temperature variations.

Say:

> I ATTRACT TO MYSELF AS THE SEED ATTRACTS SALT.
> LET MY CRYSTAL BE NOT SALT, BUT GOLD.

Over time, you will observe the seed crystal attracting salt from the solution and growing. As some water naturally evaporates, you will also observe the brine solution decreasing. Ensure this does not leave the crystal exposed by topping-up the solution if necessary.

Your work as you observe this growth is to notice how certain attitudes and expectations do appear to 'attract' abundance. This is not to be construed (as we discuss elsewhere in this course) as a law of attraction, merely that it appears to work as such.

It is true to say "like attracts like" because everything (as the Emerald tablet implies) is connected and is indeed one thing. There is only one, which is "like" itself, Universe. And you must see that **this** is the Philosopher's Stone - and the Prima Materia - which we seek by our Alchemy. The stone reflects and projects everything because it **is** everything. The lead **is** the gold.

This is the true and hidden secret of our Alchemy.

Reading 3b (General): Alchemy and Initiation

One of the most significant utilisations of alchemy in the western esoteric tradition is as a model of the initiation system. Although various alchemical authors describe different stages, steps, phases and orders of transformation and transmutation in their works, the significance of a perceivable pattern of progress is an essential underpinning to the organisation of many esoteric orders. This progress is often measured in the ten 'grades' corresponding to the Tree of Life, although the alchemical process is more often than not modelled in 7, 9 or 12 steps[65]. Here are George Ripley's twelve stages:

- The First Gate - Calcination
- The Second Gate - Solution
- The Third Gate - Separation
- The Fourth Gate - Conjunction
- The Fifth Gate - Putrefaction
- The Sixth Gate - Congelation
- The Seventh Gate - Cibation
- The Eighth Gate - Sublimation
- The Ninth Gate - Fermentation
- The Tenth Gate - Exaltation
- The Eleventh Gate - Multiplication
- The Twelfth Gate - Projection

The first two stages of Alchemy according to Ripley are Calcination and Solution. The first is described as "the reduction of the matters used to a non-metallic condition" (usually by application of gentle, external, heat). In Cavendish's interpretation of this process, he suggests," Calcination probably stands for the purging fires of aspiration and self-discipline ... The work begins with a burning discontent with oneself and one's life ... Combined with a fierce determination to do better, the result is the disintegration of the natural self. The outer, surface aspects of the personality are burned away and what is left is the 'powder' of the inner man."[66] He also equates this process to the tarot card of 'The Day of Judgement,' which when combined with its corresponding path on the diagram of the Tree of Life gives a constellation of guidance to the spiritual aspirant.

In this we also see another significance of alchemy, in translating – acting as an interface – between worldviews, in this case the esoteric and the Christian. This can be seen in Faivre's analysis of the Chemical Wedding, where he discusses the world-views of Paracelsism, non-Lutherian Hermeticism, Naturphilosophie, Christian revelation, and Neoplatonism in the context of grace and redemption, using the described pilgrimage as a vehicle for discussing the paradoxes within and between these philosophies.[67]

As Hoeller puts it, alchemy can be seen as a "modality of redemption,"[68] allowing the praxis and theoria of the work to provide mechanisms that technically are seen as belonging to the religious sphere. This reprises Hitchcock's "moral theory of alchemy" where repentance equates to philosophical contrition.[69] In fact, during the Reformation, alchemy enjoyed a resurgence as religious unity dissipated; "Alchemical symbolism provided an ideal framework for individuals seeking new schemes of salvation both for themselves and the world at large."[70]

Thus we see that alchemy is significant in providing a model –or at the very least, a template- into which the unseen transformations of consciousness can be projected, providing a mapping system on the journey to the soul. It is no surprise then, that Alchemy fits the "praxis of concordance" suggested by Faivre as a relative element of esotercism, that is to say, an attempt to cover common denominators between traditions, performing as a *philosophia perennis*.

In, "The Age of Gold," Melodini writes, "the real aim of alchemy is to attain the apotheosis of the human mind through conscious creation."[71] It is this conscious attempt to free the spirit that is the abiding driver of all gnostic or hermetic pursuit and the ability of alchemy to capture that drive which makes it a fundamental of the esoteric tradition *en masse*,

Zosimos, in "On Virtue" dreamt of an innumerable crowd of men, being boiled alive, undergoing a transmutation into pneuma, by undergoing this "punishment" (kolasis). Acording to Newman, he argued that Nature (physis) must be "forced to the investigation, whereupon she, suffering, will take on successive forms until her punishment renders her spiritual." In this sense we are both dealing with the phenonomological concerns of dynamic processes and the 'glorified through suffering' of the esoteric adept, whom in the Golden Dawn arises from initiation with the words,

"Rise, glorified by suffering. Rise, purified by humility."[72]

Luther also wrote of the correspondence between alchemical transformation and human spiritual transformation, on the *ars alchimica* he noted, "The science of Alchemy I like very well, and indeed, it is truly the natural philosophy of the ancients ... also, for the sake of the allegory and secret signification, which is exceedingly fine, touching the resurrection of the dead at the Last Day."[73]

Jung suggested that "the opus alchymicum, in spite of its chemical aspects, was always understood as a kind of rite after the manner of an opus divinum."[74] The ritual activity of alchemy, as a work whose practice changes the practitioner, and which change informs the work itself, is a fundamental assumption of initiation, whose goal is to reveal the divine essence of man in progressive stages, with identifiable step-changes. Indeed, the analogy can be seen in many chemical correspondences; the boiling of water reveals a slight loss of temperature for a moment prior to boiling, which is due to energy being taken from the heat source to break the molecular bonds. This state-change is analogous to the 'dark night of the soul' that many practitioners experience prior to significant initiatory experiences. It is a point noted by Regardie, that initiation is often preceded by breakdown, amongst others familiar with both psychoanalysis and initiation.

Praxis III

The Third Praxis - Separation

Once Solution has dissolved the inert first material of our work, which was made powdery and loose by the calcination, we can now - and only now - separate out the components of the material. In projects, when you are looking at a complex system, whether it be a family in therapy or a multi-million dollar company, you have to make clear distinctions to begin to deal with the transformation or healing work. This separation is of course, artificial, in that it is only a stage along the way. It also has to be timed correctly; try to break apart a thing until it is ready, you will shatter it, leave it too late, and it will be impossible. With separation, timing is essential.

Ripley says of this process:

> Separation does each part from the other divide,
> The subtle from the gross, the thick from the thin,
> But look you set aside manual Separation,
> For that pertains to fools that little good do win,
> But in our Separation Nature does not cease,
> Making division of qualities elemental,
> Into a fifth degree till they be turned all.

Indicating that the matter is reduced into the elemental qualities at this stage; it's fiery, earthy, airy and watery components, which are then turned to a fifth element, a spiritual one. This was not the only type of separation to be discussed by alchemists; others saw the stage of separation as resolving out the three basic components of Salt, Mercury and Sulpher. It is these three that we will explore in our third Praxis.

Meeting the Three Principles

Enter into your Alchemical body and make your way through the Portal of Vitriol into the Square of the Elements. It is here that you will meet the Three Principles of Salt, Mercury and Sulpher, firmly established in the courtyard of the elemental realm. Ask the Winged Guide to come out from the Furnace Room and enter into the courtyard (here lies an initiatory process) to assist your work.

Call upon the figure of Salt to present themselves to you.

Suggested verse:

> Open the Kingdom of Matter,
> And come forth, O Sal
> That I may know thy secret
> And work to Higher Things.

- Ask the figure: How may I transform my body?

Call upon the figure of Mercury to present themselves to you.

Suggested verse:

> Many-eyed Mercurius,
> Volatile and Quick,
> Present yourself to me
> That the medicine is created.

- Ask the figure: How may I transform my mind?

Call upon the figure of Sulpher to present themselves to you.

Suggested verse:

> Separate the venom,
> Sulpher, Oil and Fire
> Be Quick to come
> And fast to answer.

- Ask the figure: How may I transform my emotions?

Take notice of these answers in the three separate areas of body, mind and emotions - in Kabbalah, corresponding to Malkuth, Hod and Netzach. At present they are distinctly different, but we will come to find that by working alchemically, we divide in order to unite. As the magician Aleister Crowley wrote; we are "divided for the sake of union".

When you have taken these answers and thanked the figures of Salt, Mercury and Sulpher, you may choose to work with them further as suggested previously, or at the guidance of the Winged Guide. Once your work has completed, bid farewell to the figures and return through the Portal of Vitriol.

At this point in the alchemical process, you may be experiencing a distinct feeling of displacement, or a general unsettlement. We are here on the first threshold of transformation, for having made our separation we can now be assured that our elements are purged and pure, and can be re-combined for the next stage of the alchemical process. As Ripley here puts it:

> Of Separation the Gate must thus be won,
> That furthermore yet you may proceed,
> Towards the Gate of secret Conjunction,
> Into the inner Castle which will you lead,
> Do after my counsel if you will speed,
> With two strong locks this Gate is shut,
> As consequently you shall well know.

Reading 3c: The Crowning of Nature (17th Century)

In our source material reading for this third module, we look at an important alchemical work, known as the Crowning of Nature. This was written in the 17th century, and still in popular use in the 18th century. A full version of this text and the 68 illustrations which accompany it can be found on Adam Mclean's Alchemy website.

This reading should be considered with the *techne* work of this module, and the notes given therein on the secret of magickal alchemy. Notice how the ambiguity of description can be resolved if one considers the *techne* work. That the various divisions of the stone and the work are always considered as one thing, secret yet plain, and revealed in all nature and the alchemical work.

You may wish to pursue this source material and discover in what other ways the division of Universe is seen by this work.

The Crowning of Nature (Extract)

The influence of the heavens by the will and command of God, descends from above and mixes with the virtues and properties of the Stars, and likewise in this manner is the first production of our seed. You must not take it out of any combustible for it fights with it without being prejudiced, but is known out of a metallic root ordained by the Creator only for the generation of metals. You must look [for] it in the seed of its proper nature from which nature may produce it. Bernard Trevisan's books are writ true, right and once by circumstances to amuse souls.

The Elements are Water, Air, Earth, and Fire, which must be so applied and governed until such time they produce a soul. We gather the four elements by a concordance of the Seven Planets. All our work is to Congeal and Dissolve the body, and Congeal the Spirit. God being before all things, when He was alone created one Substance, which He called the first matter and of that substance he created the Elements, and from them created all things.

Our Stone is the Quintessence of the Four Elements, separated from them and reduced into a fifth Essence, being extracted out of the body of the first matter. Nature created by God prepared with human artifice, then by the Conjunction and Union of the said elements after their perfect rectification, reduces them into a fifth, a glorious fifth Essence or Spirit called Quintessence, appearing in a glorified body which is found in one only thing created by God.

Wheresoever is found a metallic Spirit, a metallic Soul and a body metallic, there is also found infallibly Quicksilver, Sulphur and Salt, in which certainly will make a perfect metallic body.

We gather it from the most perfect Creature upon which the Sun ever set his eyes. St Dunstan's work, De Occulta Philosophia E: G: I: A, calls it the food of Angels, the heavenly Viaticum, the Bread of Life, and it is undoubtedly next under God, the true Alchochodon or giver of years, and he does not so much admire the question whether any man can die that uses it, as to think why the possessors of it should desire to live, who have these manifestations of Glory and eternity represented to their fleshly eyes.

Our Stone is made or composed of Two, Three, Four, and Fire: of Five, that is the quintessence, of Four which are the Four Elements, of Three which is of three Principle natural things, of Two which signifies double mercury, and of One which is the first principle of all things, which was produced clean and pure from the Creation of the world, fiat – be it made.
There are Creatures created more noble than Gold and we must look [for] it where truth will find it, which so hath put in nature, and man cannot know it by sight, except he see the whole work.

Theoria III: Interpreting an Alchemical Image

In your Theory homework for this module, you are encouraged to take an Alchemical Image and analyse it symbolically. Although such an approach is reductive and artificial, it is a useful introduction to appreciating alchemical mandalas through contemplation.

A useful textbook for this practice is Lyndy Abraham's *Dictionary of Alchemical Imagery*. If you take the individual components of an image and list them, you will be surprised how many symbols can be found. Do not forget that even background material may be symbolic; the sky, clouds, landscape all form part of the overall image and may not be accidental.

In this illustration from Basil Valentine's Twelve Keys (1599) we see how the well-known magician and writer, A. E. Waite (1857 - 1942), a prominent member of the Hermetic Order of the Golden Dawn, interpreted the symbols. You may wish to make your own attempt at listing, identifying and contemplating the various symbols of the key before reading Waite's interpretation.

Questions for Analysis

What figures are evident in the image; do these represent known uses of figures for various elements and components, i.e. is a figure representing Saturn, or Sulpher?

What are the figures doing? What process might this represent?

Are there animals, and do these also represent processes or components?

What does the landscape suggest?

Are there natural processes being depicted, such as rain? Do these give additional clues as to the meaning of the image?

Extract from *The Pictorial Symbols of Alchemy* by A.E. Waite

This, it will be seen, is the crowned or philosophical Mercury, bearing in either hand the caduceus, which is his characteristic emblem, and having wings upon his shoulders, signifying the volatilized state. But there are also wings beneath his feet, meaning that he has overcome this state, and has been fixed by the art of the sages, which is part of the Great Work, requiring the concurrence of the Sun and Moon, whose symbols appear behind him. The figures at either side carry on their wands or swords respectively the Bird of Hermes and a crowned serpent. The latter corresponds to that serpent which, by the command of Moses, was uplifted in the wilderness for the healing of the children of Israel. As in this figure Mercury has become a constant fire, one of the figures is shielding his face from the brilliance. He is on the side of the increasing moon, but on the side of the sun is he who has attained the Medicine, and he looks therefore with a steadfast face upon the unveiled countenance of the vision. According to Basil Valentine, Mercury is the principle of life.

Here are some other symbols which you might like to interpret.

Adam MacLean (*The Alchemical Mandala*, p. 78) notes that the birds in this image may represent the four elements; Crow=Earth, Swan=Water, Peacock=Air, Phoenix=Fire.

Module 4: Conjunction

In this fourth module, we look at bringing things together, providing a conjunction of ideas, leading to further alchemical insights and discoveries. The alchemical process was a constant sorting process, a mingling of different elements, then a separating out prior to further mixing. During this process, learning takes place, insight occurs, and mystical states are produced. We see in this form of magical alchemy a series of initiations - learning experiences which lead to an increasing level of consistency and constant appreciation of Universe.

Nowhere in alchemical literature is this better discussed than in the *Chemical Wedding* (1616), one of the three so-called *Rosicrucian* manifestos, which we examine further in our praxis work of this module. However, in preparation for that work, it is recommended that you spend a week contemplating this extract from the Chemical Wedding.

In particular, consider it an allegory of awakening to the mystical path. In this context, what happens to the narrator? How does he respond? What physical and mental symptoms does he describe? When is he asleep and awake?

What is learnt from this first call to awakening?

This is the first part of the first day of the seven days described by the text, and each day of his journey to the wedding, and his experiences at the wedding, describes further alchemical and magical transformation.

Reading 4a (source): The Chemical Wedding

On an evening before Easter Day, I sat at a table, and having (as my custom was) in my humble prayer sufficiently conversed with my Creator, and considered many great mysteries (whereof the Father of Lights his Majesty had shown me not a few) and being now ready to prepare in my heart, together with my dear Paschal Lamb, a small, unleavened, undefiled cake; all of a sudden arose so horrible a tempest, that I imagined no other but that through its mighty force, the hill on which my little house was founded would fly into pieces.

But inasmuch as this, and the like from the Devil (who had done me many a spite) was no new thing to me, I took courage, and persisted in my meditation, till somebody in an unusual manner touched me on the back; whereupon I was so hugely terrified, that I dared hardly look about me; yet I showed myself as cheerful as (in such occurrences) human frailty would permit. Now the same thing still twitching me several times by the coat, I looked back, and behold it was a fair and glorious lady, whose garments were all sky-coloured, and curiously (like Heaven) bespangled with golden stars; in her right hand she bore a trumpet of beaten gold, on which a Name was engraved which I could well read but am as yet forbidden to reveal it. In her left hand she had a great bundle of letters of all languages, which she (as I afterwards understood) was to carry to all countries. She also had large and beautiful wings, full of eyes throughout, with which she could mount aloft, and fly swifter than any eagle.

I might perhaps have been able to take further notice of her, but because she stayed so little time with me, and terror and amazement still possessed me, I had to be content. For as soon as I turned about, she turned her letters over and over, and at length drew out a small one, which with great reverence she laid down upon the table, and without giving one word, departed from me. But in her mounting upward, she gave so mighty a blast on her gallant trumpet, that the whole hill echoed from it, and for a full quarter of an hour after, I could hardly hear my own words.

In so unlooked for an adventure I was at a loss, how either to advise or to assist my poor self, and therefore fell upon my knees and besought my Creator to permit nothing contrary to my eternal happiness to befall me. Whereupon with fear and trembling, I went to the letter, which was now so heavy, that had it been mere gold it could hardly have been so weighty. Now as I was diligently viewing it, I found a little seal, on which a curious cross with this inscription, IN HOC SIGNO VINCES, was engraved.

Now as soon as I espied this sign I was the more comforted, as not being ignorant that such a seal was little acceptable, and much less useful, to the Devil. Whereupon I tenderly opened the letter, and within it, in an azure field, in golden letters, found the following verses written.

This day, today
Is the Royal Wedding day.
For this thou wast born
And chosen of God for joy
Thou mayest go to the mountain
Whereon three temples stand,
And see there this affair.
Keep watch
Inspect thyself
And shouldst thou not bathe thoroughly
The Wedding may work thy bane.
Bane comes to him who faileth here
Let him beware who is too light.

Below was written : Sponsus and Sponsa.

As soon as I had read this letter, I was presently like to have fainted away, all my hair stood on end, and a cold sweat tricked down my whole body. For although I well perceived that this was the appointed wedding, of which seven years before I was acquainted in a bodily vision, and which now for so long a time I had with great earnestness awaited, and which lastly, by the account and calculation of the planets, I had most diligently observed, I found so to be, yet could I never foresee that it must happen under such grievous perilous conditions. For whereas I before imagined, that to be a welcome and acceptable guest, I needed only to be ready to appear at the wedding, I was now directed to Divine Providence, of which until this time I was never certain.

I also found by myself, the more I examined my self, that in my head there was nothing but gross misunderstanding, and blindness in mysterious things, so that I was not able to comprehend even those things which lay under my feet, and which I daily conversed with, much less that I should be born to the searching out and understanding of the secrets of Nature, since in my opinion Nature might everywhere find a more virtuous disciple, to whom to entrust her precious, though temporary and changeable, treasures.

I found also that my bodily behaviour, and outward good conversation, and brotherly love towards my neighbour, was not duly purged and cleansed. Moreover the tickling of the flesh manifested itself, whose affection was bent only to pomp and bravery, and worldly pride, and not to the good of mankind: and I was always contriving how by this art I might in a short time abundantly increase my profit and advantage, rear up stately palaces, make myself an everlasting name in the world, and other similar carnal designs. But the obscure words concerning the three temples particularly afflicted me, which I was not able to make out by any after-speculation, and perhaps should not have done so yet, had they not been wonderfully revealed to me.

Thus stuck between hope and fear, examining my self again and again, and finding only my own frailty and impotence, not being in any way able to succour myself, and exceedingly amazed at the forementioned threatening, at length I betook myself to my usual and most secure course - after I had finished my earnest and most fervent prayer, I laid myself down in my bed, so that perchance my good angel by the Divine permission might appear, and (as it had sometimes formerly happened) instruct me in this doubtful affair. Which to the praise of God, my own good, and my neighbours' faithful and hearty warning and amendment, did now likewise come about.

For I was yet scarcely fallen asleep, when I thought that I, together with an innumerable multitude of men, lay fettered with great chains in a dark dungeon, in which, without the least glimpse of light, we swarmed like bees one over another, and thus rendered each other's affliction more grievous. But although neither I nor any of the rest could see one jot, yet I continually heard one heaving himself above the other, when his chains and fetters had become ever so slightly lighter, though none of us had much reason to shove up above the other, since we were all captive wretches.

Now when I with the rest had continued a good while in this affliction, and each was still reproaching the other with his blindness and captivity, at length we heard many trumpets sounding together and kettle drums beating in such a masterly fashion, that it even revived us in our calamity and made us rejoice. During this noise the cover of the dungeon was lifted up from above, and a little light let down to us. Then first might truly have been discerned the bustle we kept, for all went pell-mell, and he who perchance had heaved himself up too much, was forced down again under the others' feet. In brief, each one strove to be uppermost. Neither did I myself linger, but with my weighty fetters slipped up from under the rest, and then heaved myself upon a stone, which I laid hold of; howbeit, I was caught at several times by others, from whom yet as well as I might, I still guarded myself with hands and feet. For we imagined no other but that we should all be set at liberty, which yet fell out quite otherwise.

For after the nobles who looked upon us from above through the hole had recreated themselves a while with our struggling and lamenting, a certain hoary-headed ancient man called to us to be quiet, and having scarcely obtained this, began (as I still remember) to speak on thus:

If the poor human race
Were not so arrogant
It would have been given much good
From my mother's heritage,
But because the human race will not take heed
It lies in such straits
And must be held in prison.
And yet my dearest mother
Will not regard their mischief,

She leaves her lovely gifts
That many a man might come to the light,
Though this may chance but seldom
That they be better prized
Nor reckoned as mere fable.

Therefore in honour of the feast
Which we shall hold today,
That her grace may be multiplied
A good work will she do :
The rope will now be lowered
Whoever may hang on to it
He shall be freed.

Techne IV

The Alchemical Adorations

These are taken from the lesser-known work of Cesare Ripa, who conceived of a dictionary of emblems and their meanings, published in 1593.[75] This was called the *Iconologia* and whilst not strictly alchemical, is a useful background text to understand how emblems were viewed at this time. You may also see the relationship to Tarot cards; the emblem for "Dominion over oneself" repeats the image of the 'Man and the Lion' common to the Visconti tarot deck of the mid-fifteenth century, although it also appears as a 'Woman and a Lion' in variants of the Tarocchi of Mantegna of about 1470.[76]

These two adorations are to be performed in the morning and evening, and mark a significant change to your way of viewing time. They should be repeated daily for the last half of this course.

The Alchemical Adoration of the Morning

Face East with a chalice of water in which you have sprinkled some salt, and, lighting a candle, say:

Let doubtful night pass,
As this light precedes the day.
By my Alchemy I greet you,
O light-bearing Star.

Pour the water as adoration, and say:

As this dawn brings summer dew,
the Frost of Winter, Autumn mist
or Spring rain
By this adoration I am transformed anew.

Spend a moment contemplating the tasks of the day, and contemplating the four elements (Air and Fire in the Candle, Earth and Water in the Chalice). Consider that the day ahead, between sun-rise and sun-set is an opportunity to re-make the world around you with every thought, word and deed. View yourself as an alchemist in the grandest laboratory of all time; Universe. How will you transfigure the day? You cannot not make change, and if you couldn't not fail, what would you do?

FIG. 75. Crepusculo della Mattina: MORNING TWI-LIGHT.

A naked Youth, of a carnation, brown Colour, Wings of the same Colour, in a Posture of mounting aloft; a splendid Star on the Crown of his Head; in his left Hand an Urn inverted, pouring out Drops of Water; in the right, a lighted Torch; a Swallow, fluttering in the Air, behind.

His Colours shew that it is *doubtful* whether he belongs to Night or Day; the Wings, that this Interval *soon* passes away. The Star is *Lucifer*, that brings Light; the Urn, that in Summer *Dew falls*, and *Hoar-frost* in Winter; the Torch, that Twi-light is the Messenger of Heaven, and always goes before the Morning. The Swallow sings *early* in the Morning.

The Alchemical Adoration of the Evening

Face West with a chalice of water in which you have sprinkled some salt, and, lighting a stick of incense, say:

Let doubtful day pass,
As this silence precedes the night
By my Alchemy I greet you,
O first-seen star of light.

Pour the water as adoration, and say:

As this evening brings peace
And memory of the day,
Clouds pass into the west,
And by this adoration I am purified.

Contemplate that you have transformed the day and now return to rest. That the events of the day are now not more than memories. Where - literally - is the day that has been? Where is it now present? As you meditate upon that thought, consider the incense as memory, purifying your self.

FIG. 78. Crepufculo della Sera : *EVENING TWI-LIGHT.*
He is but a Babe ftill, wing'd; of a duskifh carnation Colour, in a Pofture of flying towards the Weft; a bright Star on his Head; in his right Hand holds an Arrow, and in his left a Bat.
His *flying* fhews it to be the Evening Twi-light. The Star is *Hefperus.* The Arrow fignifies the Vapours attracted by the Sun, which having nothing to fuftain them, fall down, and are more or lefs noxious, according to Places high, or low.

Reading 4b (General): Theoretical and Practical Alchemy

This distinction between practical and psychological may be entirely contemporary. Domenico Beccafumi, also known as Meracino or Mecuccio, working in the early decades of the 16th century in Siena, was both artist and alchemist. In a series of woodcuts thought to be amongst the earliest printed depictions of alchemical imagery, dating in the period 1525-1540, the alchemist is both practitioner *and* philosopher.[77] They show a process in which the philosopher-alchemist and the laboratory worker-alchemist begin by finding the seven metals, personified as Greek Gods buried in the mountains, gathering these and leading them through a transformation process in the laboratory.

Although the two figures are shown in the series as separate, in a way they also seem to be one and the same - merely two different aspects of the alchemist.

That the alchemical process is an internal process as well as an external process is intimated by Daniel Mogling (under the pseudonym of Theophilus Schweighardt) in *The Mirror of the Wisdom of the Rosicrucians* (1616). Here we see that although there are three aspects of the alchemical work; the *'ora'* or prayer, the *'labora'* in fields and streams, and the *'atte natura'* or examination of nature in the workshop, divided into both a primary and secondary work (*'ergon et parergon'*) that the hidden skull symbolism and the textual reference to "climb down from the mountain and look with thy left eye (but with the right eye maintaining its precedence) into time and the creatures" both suggest changes in the state or awareness of the alchemist.[78] Indeed, Mogling furthermore stresses, "'Know Thyself!','Know Thyself! I say, and so thou shalt come to pansophic perfection ..."[79]

This movement to a pansophic working of Alchemy is also evident in Heinrich Khunrath (1560 - 1601), whose *Amphitheatre of Eternal Wisdom* depicts a place of working where the laboratory has become a *lab-oratorium*; a place of prayer and meditation. This interpretation of alchemy as an entirely spiritual art, to the contemporary academic Allison Coudert, marks Khunrath as a "spiritual extremist" and "clearly unbalanced".[80]

It is argued in this course that although there may be little case for the *entirety* of alchemical pursuits to be other than coded references to physical transformations, a number of alchemists themselves testified to the psychological elements of their business through dream and vision. Indeed, contemporary chemists have benefited from this dialogue of practical work and imagination.

Friedrich August Kekulé von Stradonitz (1829-1896), who discovered the structure of the Benzene molecule is in this lineage of chemists who have worked in dreams;

"...I was sitting writing on my textbook, but the work did not progress; my thoughts were elsewhere. I turned my chair to the fire and dozed. Again the atoms were gamboling before my eyes. This time the smaller groups kept modestly in the background. My mental eye, rendered more acute by the repeated visions of the kind, could now distinguish larger structures of manifold conformation; long rows sometimes more closely fitted together all twining and twisting in snake-like motion. But look! What was that? One of the snakes had seized hold of its own tail, and the form whirled mockingly before my eyes. As if by a flash of lightning I awoke; and this time also I spent the rest of the night in working out the consequences of the hypothesis".

Illus. Plate 6 from *the Book of Lambspring* (1625)[81]

It is attributed to Kekulé that he told colleagues "let us learn to dream!"[82]

Reading 4c (Academic): Alchemy & Psychology

The psychoanalyst C. G. Jung wrote extensively on alchemy and had a large collection of alchemical and Gnostic works. He wrote that alchemy provided evidence of his own inner experience, historically preconfigured;

> If I had not succeeded in finding such evidence, I would never have been able to substantiate my ideas. Therefore, my encounter with alchemy was decisive for me, as it provided me with the historical basis which I hitherto lacked.[83]

Jung's pursuit of the parallels between depth psychology ('analytical psychology') and alchemy started in 1928, when Richard Wilhelm sent Jung his translation of *The Secret of the Golden Flower*, a Chinese Taoist text.[84] Following the lack of material and research in this area, Jung came to write a significant amount of material on alchemy, notably *Alchemical Studies* and *Psychology and Alchemy*.[85]

To Jung, the imagination was the key to the secret of nature in alchemy, and the secret of the self in analytical psychology; "The *imaginatio*, as the alchemists understand it, is in truth a key that opens the door to the secret of the Opus".[86]

The role of imagination in alchemy has been touched on by many authors and scholars; Karen-Claire Voss provides a summary including C. G. Jung, Marie Louise von Franz, Henry Corbin, Gaston Bachelard, Gilbert Durand and Antoine Faivre.[87]

Other post-Jungian Psychotherapists have continued to mine the rich ore of alchemical symbolism for the gold of the whole psyche[88]; Marie Louise von Franz, Edward Edinger, Jeffrey Raff, Joseph L. Henderson and Dyane N. Sherwood have all contributed to the exposition of alchemical iconography as "protean mythologem and the shimmering symbol" of the development of the psyche[89].

In parallel to Jung, the Viennese psychologist Herbert Silberer (1882 - 1923) also treated the parallels between alchemical symbolism and the dream-state[90]. He had also, in 1919, written a text on the hypnagogic state. In his analysis of the alchemical parable, the *Parabola of Madathanus*[91] (attributed to Adrian Seumenicht, c. 1621)[92] included in his master-work, *Probleme der Mystik und ihrer Symbolik* (Problems of Mysticism and its Symbolism) he wrote;

> In the narrative we have just examined its dream-like character is quite noticeable. On what does it depend? Evidently the parable must bear marks that are peculiar to the dream. In looking for correspondences we discover them even upon superficial examination. Most noticeable is the complete and sudden change of place ...[93]

He goes on to list other correspondences - "peculiarities of representation"[94] unique to both dream and hermetic text - such as unmediated knowledge, unexpected uncertainties in the narrator's character and appraisal of the environment, and the presence of motifs such as obstacles, difficulties, passages and paths common to both dreamer and alchemist.

Silberer was not alone in pre-dating Jung and Freud in exploring the relationship of esotericism and psychology; the occultist Wilhelm Fliess[95] worked alongside Freud[96] in the period 1887 - 1902, Carl Gustav Carus pre-dated Jung in his conceptualisation of the human unconscious and its link to the conscious mind of God, the *Naturphilosopher* Schelling, and Gotthilf Heinrich Schubert all treated the mechanism of dreams and images as emancipatory devices.[97]

To Jung also, alchemy was a rich source of psychological material projected from the unconscious. He wrote:

> The real nature of matter was unknown to the alchemist: he knew it only in hints. In seeking to explore it he projected the unconsciousness into the darkness of matter in order to illuminate it. In order to explain the mystery of matter he projected yet another mystery - his own unknown psychic background - into what was to be explained ... This procedure was not, of course, intentional; it was an involuntary occurrence.[98]

However, this proposal was taken in many quarters as comprehending the *whole* of the alchemical endeavour; even by the mid-1900's alchemy was being treated by some as an entirely psychological and spiritual pursuit:

> Can scientific sense be made out of the labour of the alchemists, most of which was symbolism and definitely *not* chemical experiment? The ancients knew what chemical processes were, and therefore could not overlook the most of what they did was not chemistry.[99]

Theoria IV: Essays and Articles

At this stage of your working through this six-month course, you are encouraged to prepare your own article or essay on the alchemical works. This is a test of your approach to alchemy and your ability to focus on a particular aspect of the vast subject matter. You are encouraged to send your work at this stage to the author/mentor of this course for comment, if you would like feedback at this stage. It is suggested that your work is between 4-12 pages of text, with additional footnotes, book list or link references.

Your work may be sent to adept@farawaycentre.com for feedback.

Suitable questions for your consideration include:

- How do the stages of Alchemy differ between two specific writers? Choose two writers whose work is available to you, and who have written about the stages of alchemy.

- What do the colour changes of Putrefaction symbolize, in the words of several alchemists? These are the colours white, red and black; referred to as albedo, rubedo and nigredo.

- What are the key works of Alchemy between the 17th and 18th centuries? How do various authors develop earlier ideas?

- How does Christianity (or Kabbalah) influence Alchemical thought in the works of two specific writers?

- Explain and explore a small series of emblems or illustrations, using symbolic analysis. You may choose a particular sequence, such as the *Mutus Liber*, or *Keys* of Basil Valentine, although you may wish to explore only an extract of several images if the sequence has many images.

- What are the qualities of Salt, Mercury and Sulpher?

- Find as many references as you can to the definition of the Philosopher's Stone in alchemical source materials. What do they have in common, or where do they markedly differ?

Most importantly with this work, follow what interests you and what speaks to you; alchemy is a living art, and should be pursued with all your interest engaged fully. It is also important to read source materials where possible rather than post-modern interpretations, imaging that the alchemist is actually talking to you directly - you may hear a very different message.

Praxis IV
The Fourth Praxis - Conjunction

Many alchemical diagrams and illustrations refer to a marriage. This symbol of union is common across many hermetic texts, often between a King and a Queen. In this fourth stage of Conjunction, the image arises as a wedding between a King and Queen. However, this illustration holds more secrets in the symbolism. The two-headed Janus, for example, is depicted on the top of the alchemical furnace, which we met in Calcination. This symbolises the two-fold nature of the work; inner and outer. It may also be taken as a symbol that this work now begins to take on a life of its own, transcending our usual notions of time. You may find curious coincidences starting to happen as you make this conjunction. Things will literally, just start to "come together".

Inside the furnace burns now the secret fire, which we created in Solution. The fire is now secret, within, not burning as it was when first it was encountered.

The figure of Neptune is enigmatic; but a look at his three-pronged trident reveals that he is symbolic of the Alchemical Water conjoining the three principles of Salt, Mercury and Sulpher that were separated out in our previous praxis.

The rainbow - Queseth, in Hebrew and Kabbalah, meaning both bow and bridge - forms a uniting bridge between the powers and influences of the Solar and Lunar realms. In Norse myth, the rainbow also functioned as a bridge between the higher and lower worlds. As we see, this image contains many illustrations of conjunction. However, it remains that there are two distinct things being conjoined together - they have not become one as yet. This is for a later part of the Work.

The most famous example of the wedding symbolism in alchemy is that used in the Rosicrucian text, the *Chymical Wedding*, the third of three "Rosicrucian Manifestos" published in Germany between 1614-16. These three pamphlets were the *Fama Fraternitatis* (1614), the *Confessio Fraternitatis* (1615), and the *Chymical Wedding* (1616). They were the start of the Rosicrucian myth which endures to the present time in organisations such as AMORC.

You have already read an extract from the *Chemical Wedding* as the first reading of this module.

Although published anonymously, it is now widely accepted that the manifestos originated in the "Learned and Christian Society" established by Johann Valentin Andreae in Tübingen in 1610[100]. This group also comprised of Chrisoph Besold and Tobias Hess – it is likely the manifestos were the result of a meeting of these minds, although Andreae did claim authorship of the Chemical Wedding. It has been reasonably suggested that as Andreae was aged only nineteen at the time of the writing of this latter text, on the evidence of its more mature construction and content, compared with other works by Andreae, it was likely re-worked by the group prior to actual publication[101].

Illus.1 Johann Valentin Andreae (1586-1642)[102]

Incidentally, the first appearance of the word 'Rosenkreuz' in a printed book was in a Tyrolean schoolmaster's response to the unpublished *Fama*, in 1612[103]. This schoolmaster, musician and alchemist, Adam Haselmeyer, was deeply versed in the works of Paracelsus, and proclaimed a newly-founded religion, the 'Theosphrastia Sancta'.

These three texts, particularly the *Chymical Wedding*, are a wealth of alchemical, allegorical and symbolic mysticism, and are worth your further study if you wish to go beyond this present praxis.

The Wedding Day

Enter into your Alchemical body and make your way through the Portal of Vitriol into the Square of the Elements. As you pass into the Alchemical Garden, notice that it is bedecked and decorated with all manner of roses and garlands, in preparation for a royal wedding. Hear music such as church bells in the distance, and the sound of singing as you walk through to the elemental square at the centre of the garden.

You should find the Winged Guide in the Square awaiting for you. If he is not present, find him in the Furnace Room and ask him to accompany you to the Square.

At this stage of your Praxis, you should be able to follow the course of events without too much further instruction. However, the structure must have a number of key components, which you should endeavour to follow. Firstly, there should be an Invitation. The Guide may give this to you, or some other figure. There will then be a Journey to the place of the Wedding. You may encounter some obstacles or other events on the way.

When you arrive at the place of the Wedding, there will be a Mediator figure, who will bring together the two halves of the marriage. You may find yourself surprised by who or what is brought together in your unique Wedding. Although it should not be any persons known to you, living or dead - this must remain a working of images from within yourself, not confused with outer figures or your projections of those known to you.

You will be expected to give a Gift to the Wedding, and you may in fact receive a Gift from the figures being married. There may be advice given to you, or your Guide may ask you to give advice to the figures being married.

At this stage, you should be able to engage with your praxis in an imaginative and creative exercise that will have profound impact on your sense of wholeness and well-being. If combined with the other Workings in this *Entrance to the Amphitheatre* course, at this stage you will be finding yourself radically more unified with the world of events in a constant alchemical wedding of your own making.

Following on the next page is an example of a Tarot-based Wedding Journey which may inspire your own symbolic alchemical wedding.

The Wedding Day

Closing your eyes now, you feel yourself standing in a simple room, clearly lit, with a plain black floor, looking out through your own eyes as you relax in the room around you. Ahead of you is a single door upon which is depicted the Tarot card of the Universe.

The air smells dry and stale, the walls of the room are cool to the touch, and the room is utterly silent aside from the sound of your deepening breathing as you allow yourself to relax and allow the detail of the room to build around you. And as the details of the Universe card become clearer ahead of you, the door opens and the strangely garbed figure of the Fool enters the room. He gives you a stick and a bag, and asks if you would like to accompany him on his journey. Almost without giving you time to answer, he turns and dances out through the door.

Choosing to follow him, you step through the door and find yourself in a rainbow coloured room, in the centre of which is a complicated clockwork machine, in constant movement and making a dinning cacophony of sounds and noises. The Fool tells you that this is a vision of the machinery of the Universe, and as you examine the contraption more closely, you see that it is powered by motes of light, seemingly flashing in and out of existence – randomly - within the confines of the machine.

On the other side of the machinery is a single door, this one upon which is painted the Last Judgement card. The Fool takes your hand and leads you through this door, into a long chamber full of fire, but as you pass through it seems that the fire passes through you and within you, purifying you, burning away all the unwanted thoughts and emotions that restricted you in the past, leaving you feeling sharp and pure and focused. The Fool laughs as the sound of a Trumpet urges you forward. At last you reach the end of the chamber where a large arched gateway is decorated with the card of the Sun.

"Onwards!" laughs the Fool as you enter through the gateway into a sunlit meadow. Feeling the sun high above you, glowing warmly down on your skin, you pass across the meadow until you come to a great wall, engraved with the signs of the Zodiac. The Fool shows you how to climb this wall, but you find that you have to leave your shoes behind to get a grip upon the wall with your bare feet.

On the other side of the wall you drop into a twilight garden, where pale moonlight filters through the passing clouds above. As you walk the garden path, the Fool pauses by a pool, and looking at his reflection jokes, "Mirror, Mirror on the floor, who is the most foolish of us all?". You cross the garden and begin to leave it further behind as you make your way up steeper wilder slopes, towards a very bright Star in the sky ahead.

"Onwards!" yells the Fool as you reach the top of the slopes and lightning begins to play around you in the night sky. Further up the path you see a Tower struck by lightning, and avoid the toppling masonry that falls around you. You get the impression that the tower is often rebuilt only to suffer the same fate time and time again. Your path now leads into the mountains and you arrive at a cave entrance. "Down we go!" cries the Fool, as you descend into the dark underworld through a long tunnel.

The tunnel is suddenly blocked by the hulking figure of the Devil, who glares down at you with malice and anger. "Give him the food," whispers the Fool, and you reach into your sack, having perhaps forgotten it was there, to find some food which you can offer the Devil. This you do, and the Devil lets you pass after ensuring that your bag is now completely empty. "That always fools Him," says the Fool in a conspiratorial whisper, "He can never know where we're going, so he always thinks he's in charge and getting the best deal. Little does He know!"

Going further down now, following the Fool down carved steps into the dark, you come to a flooded cave where you have to cross a narrow bridge, with one foot in water which runs down one side of the bridge, and one foot on the dry side of the bridge. A deep gorge opens both sides as you make your way carefully forwards. The Fool suggests that you use your stick to balance, like a tightrope walker. "You see," he says, "couldn't have done that with a full sack on just one end, could you?"

The bridge enters into a low tunnel from which the water flows. The Fool tells you to take off any jewellery you might be wearing, or otherwise you will drown at this point. Once you have done so, you can enter the flooded tunnel and begin to swim up the stream, finally coming out the open air and sunshine again.

"Onwards!" smiles the Fool. You walk through a beautiful landscape in which everything is as perfect as you could possibly imagine a place to be. "Just like a Vision of Beauty," adds the Fool. A moment later, you come across a crowd of people, surrounding a man hanging by his feet from a noose tied from a tree. A judge sits in front of the figure, and the crowd are silent, awaiting his verdict. But the hanging figure looks at you and you see a strange peace and understanding in his eyes, which he shares with you. The Judge spins a roulette wheel on a table in front of him, and the ball falls into number twenty-three. The crowd cheer, but the Fool takes your hand and leads you away before you can see what the result means.

You continue to walk through the idyllic landscape, until you begin to rise up into hills and mountains again. A bright light appears on the path high above you. "That guy again," says the Fool, "you can never see him, because he's always ahead leading the way. I guess he's more interested in people getting to where they need to go, not just following to find him."

"Onwards!" continues the Fool. Passing through the mountains safely, you enter a rough terrain with wild plains surrounding you. Suddenly, after a moment of walking you are surprised and trapped by lions. They snarl and roar, but the Fool just grins inanely at them. He seems to have gone through all this before. As you stand, a beautiful woman approaches and smiles at the Fool, and at you, and then reaches down and quiets the lions. She points out some directions to the Fool, then walks away, the lions following her, purring like kittens. "She has that effect on me, sometimes," the Fool muses, but then, "Onwards! Onwards! Mustn't stop, even for Her!" With this, he takes you a little further across the plains until you reach a Chariot, where an armoured knight sits waiting, two sphinxes reined ahead of him, waiting for you to step up with the Fool onto the chariot. As soon as you do, the Chariot races ahead, across the plains towards a great walled city in the distance.

"Soon be there!" shouts the Fool. You enter the city, and pass through streets lined with celebrating people – there appears to be a royal wedding taking place today. "To the Inner Court," the Fool yells excitedly, "I'm expected and so are you!" The Chariot brings you to the front of a great palace, and you dismount to press your way through throngs of celebrating people, perhaps recognizing a face here and there from your past, and then from your present, and even seeing faces that you have yet to meet. You realize that the city is composed of everyone that has had some bearing on your life, and that here in this place they all have a part they play, small and large. The Fool says, "Yes, but the best thing is that the city is dancing!"

At last you come to the gate of a great inner palace, built on a carved mountain in the very centre of the city. You are stopped by a High Priest, but the Fool engages him in jesting conversation, and as he is distracted, you sneak past him. A moment later, the Fool rejoins you. "Good man," he says, "but takes things too seriously and can miss the action sometimes, but he has a lot to say when you're ready to listen."

"Oh!" continued the Fool, "but it's almost time!" as you enter the inner courtroom of the palace. Nobles and Merchants line the courtroom, forming a long corridor through which you proceed. As you walk down the line, you see ahead of you the Emperor and Empress of All Things, sat on thrones, radiating intense power and love. Behind them you sense the even more powerful energy of the Magician, and the more lovely mystery of the High Priestess, but they appear content at this time to remain less visible.

The Fool approaches the royal couple and speaks clearly, "Congratulations on your Wedding, and the harmony you bring to the Universe!" He continues, "and for my gift, on this day of unity and joy, I have brought you," and with this he pauses, turns and winks at you, "I have brought ... my SELF!"

The Fool, with this word, gives you a final smile, and claps his hands sharply, once, together. For a moment, you sense the entire scene expand outwards, encompassing the thrones, the palace, the city, the mountains, plains, caves and chambers, all the way to the door of the Universe through which you first began, and then the entire vision is drawn backwards to a single point that is at once everywhere within you and outside you ... and nowhere now ...

... that you slowly become aware of your body in a time that is now, and return comfortably in your own time to open your eyes bringing all that you have learnt with you ...

Primary Influences

Crowley, A., *The Wake World* (published in *Konx Om Pax*) Good version with original key at http://www.hermetic.com/crowley/libers/lib95.html

Ashcroft-Nowicki, D., *The Shining Paths*

Andreae, Johann Valentin, *Chymical Wedding of Christian Rosenkreutz*. See particularly *Commentary on the Chymical Wedding* by Gareth Knight and Adam Mclean).

Also, version at http://www.levity.com/alchemy/chymwed1.html

Campanella, T., *The City of the Sun*

Version at http://www.levity.com/alchemy/citysun.html

In this module we have seen how the image of the wedding, of principles coming together, provides an image of conjunction. In our workings and readings we have seen how our apparent external life and our dream life are inextricably woven together, and how alchemy hastens their conjunction. We have also seen how the theoretical and practical aspects of alchemy were not separated by practitioners, and as a result, we are encouraged to see inner lessons in outside observations, and lessons for outside in our inner observations.

So ...

> Proceed therefore unto another wall,
> Of this strong Castle of our Wisdom,
> That in at the fifth Gate you may come.

Module 5: Putrefaction

Like the Death card in the Tarot Major Arcana, the process of putrefaction is initially unwelcome to the alchemical process. It is symbolized by death and decay, skulls, skeletons and ravens. However, it is always an indication of immanent change, and for those who have followed the work of the course and perhaps are despairing of change, or experiencing doubt and difficult, this penultimate module will assist the transition to positive results.

You may like to consider the magical formula of IAO, Isis - Apophis - Osiris, as given by both Crowley and Regardie, for further elucidation of this aspect of the alchemical process.

Reading 5a (General): Alchemy and the Hypnagogic State

The engagement of the unconscious is evident in the writings of the alchemists; like those in psychotherapeutic analysis, they record the occurrence of vivid symbolic dreams and visions; Jung was aware of this[104], writing that "the alchemists themselves testify to the occurrence of dreams and visions during the Opus".[105] Jung references Nazari, the *Visio Arislei*, Ostanes, Senior, Krates, Ventura and Khunrath all as acknowledging dreams as important sources of revelation.

This activation of the unconscious is evident in as early a text as the *Visions of Zosimos* (c. 300 AD) to the literary construct of *The Alchemical Wedding* by J. V. Andreae (1616) which we have encountered already in this course.

Compare the following two accounts from these works:

> And having had this vision I awoke again and I said to myself 'what is the occasion of this vision?'[106]

and

> Whereupon the trumpets began to sound again, which gave me such a shock that I woke up, and then perceived that it was only a dream, but it so strongly impressed my imagination that I was still perpetually troubled about it, and I thought I still felt the wounds upon my feet.[107]

Or the poetic account given in the alchemical text, *John Datin's Dream*, published by Elias Ashmole (1652), which indicates the same state - which is not so much dream-like (asleep) as more specifically a *hypnagogic* state;

> Not yet full sleping, nor yet full waking,
> But betweene twayne lying in a traunce;
> Halfe closed mine Eyne in my slumbering...[108]

The term "hypnagogic" is derived from the French word *hypnagogique*, coined by the 19th century French psychologist Louis Ferdinand Alfred Maury from the Greek words *hupnos*, meaning sleep, and *agogos*, meaning leading. Frederic William Henry Myers coined the complementary term *hypnopompic*, from *hupnos* and *pompe*, meaning sending away.[109]

Both esotericist and psychologist have mined this boundary layer between sleep and wakefulness; P. D. Ouspensky (1878 - 1947), the 19th-century French Orientalist and dream diarist, Hervey de Saint-Denys (1822 - 1892) and the Freudian psychologist Herbert Silberer (1882 - 1923) all recounted profound experiences in such states.

The Danish philosopher Jurij Moskvitin concludes;

> If we remember that the essential difference between what we call the real world and the world of imagination and hallucination, is not the elements of which we build them up but the sequence in which these elements appear... then it follows that the sequences directed from without represent a limitation of the otherwise unlimited combinations of the selective forms released at random from within.[110]

In terms of the iconography of alchemy and the psychotherapeutic framework of Jung, it is notable that the images of the hypnagogic state and alchemy bear remarkable characteristics, as much as between the dream-state and alchemical imagery. Although hypnagogic and hypnopompic imagery are characterised by their variety, Mavromatis (1987) has modified Leaning's (1925) classification scheme and identified six recurrent themes:

- Formless   (waves, clouds of colour, etc.)
- Designs   (geometric and symmetrical patterns and shapes)
- Faces   (figures, animals, objects)
- Nature scenes   (landscapes, seascapes, gardens)
- Scenes with people (known personages, living, dead, unknown people)
- Print and writing (in real or imaginary languages)[111]

We see such imagery in such alchemical texts and icons as this, from the Golden Age Restored (1625);

> ...after pondering over it for some time my eyes were opened, just as happened with the two disciples at Emmaus who knew the Lord in the Breaking of Bread, and my heart burned within me. But I laid down and began to sleep. And, lo, in my dream King Solomon appeared to me in all his might, wealth, and glory, leading beside him all the women of his harem: there were threescore queens, and fourscore concubines, and virgins without number, but one was his gentle dove, most beautiful and dearest to his heart, and according to Catholic custom she held a magnificent procession wherein the Centrum was highly honoured and cherished, and its name was like an out-ointment, the fragrance of which surpassed all spices. And its fiery spirit was a key to open the temple, to enter the Holy Place, and to grasp the horns of the altar.[112]

Similarly, the six themes are evident in such images as the third emblem from the *Philosophia Reformata* of Mylius (1622). Here we see the shape of the three-headed snake appearing in the superimposed fore-ground of the image, clouds, figures, animals, the Sun and Moon as persons, and icons of nature such as the sprouting tree-stump and the mature tree as its counter-part on the right.

It has also been noted that the hypnagogic state often brings with a sense of a presence *outside* of the individual. There are particular emblems in alchemical literature that incorporate the presence of a guide, often as a representation of Hermes Trismegestus, as from this image from *The Hermetic Garden of Daniel Stolcius* (1624)[113]

Or this image of the Guide Figure from the *Book of Lambspring* (1625):

In even earlier texts, the guide - or sense of another presence outside the alchemist - is present, as in Zosimos, (whose work we will see elsewhere in this course) where is encountered "a little man, a barber, whitened by years," who responds to the question of his identity by describing himself as "a spirit and a guardian of spirits".[114]

Techne V: An Alchemical Ritual

For your penultimate working, you will engage in a ritual activity modeled around the four elements and the three main components of Alchemy that have now become familiar to you through your *Praxis* workings. It may be beneficial to revisit the third praxis prior to conducting this ritual, in order to ensure you have established a working connection with the principles of Salt, Mercury and Sulpher.

This ritual is designed to activate the basic alchemical components to effect great change in your life - positive alchemy. If you perform this ritual you may experience a subtle or dramatic change in the stability of your life - be aware that although this will be positive, it may be challenging.

The Ritual of the Divine Dew

Requirements for the Operation

You should have a place of working which is sufficient for you to walk around a small circle, with a table or altar in the centre of the working space. On the altar should be drawn a triangle, at the point of which place three small containers or pitchers/jugs. These should contain salt-water, using the salt crystals you have already created in previous course-work, and dew collected in the early morning at dawn, preferably after the night of the full moon.

In the centre of the triangle should be placed a bowl, which has sufficient capacity to hold the combined salt-water from all three pitchers. If this bowl is golden coloured, this is more suitable. It should certainly be circular.

It is optional that you may have a light above the altar and one on the altar, such as a candle. These should be contemplated when you make the statement "That which is below …"

You should also have a stick of incense, preferably myrrh or frankincense.

Preliminary Rite

Draw a circle around your place of working.

Say:

> That which is below is like that which is on high, and that which is on high is like that which is below; by these things are made the miracles of one thing.

Draw another circle above your altar.

Say:

> THE SUN IS MY FATHER, THE MOON IS MY MOTHER.

Visualise a Solar Disc about your feet, cradled in a lunar crescent.

Take Salt and Water from one of the pitchers and sprinkle the circle, saying:

> LET ME BE THE VERY PRIEST(ESS) AMONGST THE FOREMOST, GUIDING THE WORKS OF FIRE, SPRINKLING WITH THE COAGULATED WAVES OF THE DEEP-ECHOING SEA.[‡]

This purifies the place of working, removing from it all hindrances.

[‡] A more accurate translation from the Greek of the Chaldean Oracles which is often misquoted. This translation is in *Hekate Soteira*, by Sara Iles Johnston. The salt-water becomes the coagulation of the sea, so the wording is very fitting for alchemical rites.

The Ceremony

Circle the place of working with incense, saying:

> I CARRY THE PERFUME AS THE CLOUD CARRIES THE DISTILLATION OF THE WATER OF EARTH.

Circle the place of working, again sprinkling salt-water, saying:

> I SPRINKLE WITH THE LUSTRAL WATERS AS THE CLOUDS SHED RAIN AND THE DEW IS UPON THE EARTH.

Hold up the bowl upon the Altar and say:

> LET ME INVOKE NOW THE POWERS OF THE ELEMENTS UPON THIS RITE, WHICH IS DEDICATED TO THE TRANSFORMATION OF THE ONE TRUE STONE.

Return the bowl to the altar.

Face each Quarter in Turn, saying at each Quarter:

> I INVOKE THE POWERS OF THE ELEMENTS UPON THIS RITE, THAT THEY MAY BRING POSITIVE INTENT IN EACH REALM OF EARTH, AIR, FIRE AND WATER TO THIS WORKING.

Draw a triangle upon the altar with your hand, following the triangle which is already present on the altar. At each of the points there should be placed a small pitcher of salt-water. In the centre of the triangle is the bowl.

The Invocation

Pour the first pitcher into the bowl, saying, in a solid, deep, voice:

> By Salt I combine and transform.
> By Salt threefold I create change.
> By Salt I prepare and provoke.

Meditate for a moment on the material components of your life; your property, money, car, possessions, clothes and body. Imagine that these are inert, lifeless, lumps of matter with no animation. See that everything freeze-frames into a single, crystallised picture of matter, of which you and everything is a part.

Pour the second pitcher into the bowl, saying, in a whispery, light voice:

> By Mercury I inspire and animate.
> By Mercury threefold I create movement.
> By Mercury I free and release.

Meditate now for a moment on the passing of time. Hear any sounds that indicate how time is passing, wait, and respect your own feelings as you wait. Do you feel impatient, calm, in a hurry, or still? How do you continue to move in time? Do you have all the time in the world, or no time at all?

Pour the third pitcher into the bowl, saying, in a strident, commanding, voice:

> By Sulpher I inflame and transmute.
> By Sulpher threefold I create gold.
> By Sulpher I cleanse and ascend.

Now hold the bowl up and invoke:

> By my threefold art of alchemy
> I invoke the mystical marriage of elements
> I invoke change, movement and gold
> To renew my magical life.

You may now take an extract from the bowl and place it in a special bottle or container, which you should take a drop from for a full lunar cycle of twenty-eight days or until the effect is realised.

Circle the place of working with incense, saying:

> I CARRY THE PERFUME AS THE CLOUD CARRIES THE DISTILLATION OF THE WATER OF EARTH.

Circle the place of working, again sprinkling salt-water, saying:

> I SPRINKLE WITH THE LUSTRAL WATERS AS THE CLOUDS SHED RAIN AND THE DEW IS UPON THE EARTH.

Draw the circle to close the place of working, and say:

> THE OPERATION OF THE SUN IS COMPLETE.

Reading 5b (Academic): Going beyond the Grain

Paracelsus and the Art of Vulcan

Paracelsus (1493 – 1541) was born *Philippus Aureolus Theophrastus Bombastus* at Einsiedeln in Switzerland. He became known as *Paracelsus* (i.e. 'surpassing Celsus', a Roman writer on medicine) from about 1529, when he was aged thirty-six. He wrote extensively on medicine, philosophy and alchemy, which he saw as a healing art to cure disease and prolong life.

He was often criticised, led a wandering life, and had to defend his ideas against both church and state. He was undaunted, however, and believed that his ideas would long outlast him; in one of his major writings, the *Paragranum* (1529 – 30) he wrote that "I shall put forth leaves, while you will be dry fig trees".

It is this idea that we shall consider in regard of Paracelsus, who is now considered the father of Homeopathy and a forerunner in the practice of surgical wound treatment! How does a seed outlast us? How does the alchemy of an idea germinate?

For this practice, you will simply need to find a seed which you can plant; it could also be a bulb or other germinated plant. At the same time, consider a project that you are engaged in, or about to start. At the time you start the project, or wish to re-energise your activity, plant the seed. As you tend the seed, and the plant that issues from it, consider it as your project.

The two activities have a correspondence as a creative act; a manifestation in time and space. This alchemical growth can be witnessed in both plant and project, but we must consider another idea to truly go 'beyond the grain' - which is what *Paragranum* means. We must mediate upon our own mortality.

Alchemy often contains images, symbols and scenes of death and putrefaction. The image of a black raven, skull or skeleton reminds us of mortality. Some alchemical pictures show the Last Judgement, with corpses rising from tombs. There are often images of transformation; a King dying and becoming reborn, or lead turning into gold.

The work of the Alchemist is seen by Paracelsus as the art of Vulcan, the Roman God of the Forge, who was originally seen as God of both beneficial and hindering fire. Paracelsus sees the whole of creation as being created from a seed, in which the "purpose of its use and function is inherent from the beginning". However, because nothing is finished, Vulcan – the alchemist – you – must bring all things to their completion. As Paracelsus says, wood does not transform itself into boards or charcoal, neither does clay of itself become a pot.

So consider your Contemplation of Vulcan as you observe your growing plant:

1. What seed(s) have you planted?
2. What grows from this seed?
3. How does it branch out – what consequences, and to whom?
4. What aspects of growth happen naturally, and what require your work?
5. How will this growth outlast you?

In this emblem from the *Hermetic Garden*, (Daniel Stoclius, 17thC) we see a picture of the 'seed of metals'. The figure also holds a three-headed serpent, which could be taken as a symbol of growth, knowledge and divergent paths. In the sky, a lion is seen with a band of stars encompassing it, perhaps indicating the passage of time.

And, having completed this contemplation a number of times (say, daily, over a week) as your work perform the following as a Willed, Alchemical Act:

1. Consider your own death
2. Think of one thing that you would like to have outlasted you.
3. Plant the seed of that thing
4. Nurture it and tend it.

Diego Velázquez, The Forge of Vulcan (1630)
Oil on canvas, 223 x 290 cm (87 3/4 x 114 1/8 in), Museo del Prado, Madrid

Praxis V

The Fifth Praxis - Putrefaction

As well as the wedding image being common in alchemy, another event or process is also found throughout alchemical images, that of death or putrefaction. The transformative process of death is often depicted in three or four phases, represented by colours; a blackening, reddening, and whitening followed by a multi-coloured stage as colourful as the feathers of a peacock. These three phases of transformation are called by their Latin names, *nigredo, rubedo, albedo* and *Cauda Pavonis*, the peacock feathers.

Here we will only consider the image of Death as a singular process, that of putrefaction. This stage, although seen by many as fearful, is in fact essential to all workings of nature. As Ripley has it:

> And likewise unless the matter putrefy,
> It may in no way truly be altered.

To the Alchemist, Death is merely a stage in a process, in fact, here in Ripley's system it is only the fifth stage of twelve.

The Way of the Seven Steps

Enter into your Alchemical Body and pass through the Gate of Vitriol. Find that the Alchemical Garden is in a state of decay; leaves are fallen and rotting on the floor, the sky is dark, a deathly silence resides where there used to be distant sounds of song, and black wreaths are strewn about the paths.

Pass into the Square of the Elements but find nothing there other than long shadows. Feel the emptiness of the place as a physical loss. Search for anything that remains but find nothing other than a sword, which you should take up and hold. What do you feel when holding this weapon?

Now look about the garden and see that there is a small stone pyramid, with seven steps leading to the flat top of the pyramid, upon which you can see a large sacrificial bowl. Approach the base of the steps and find yourself confronted by a large snake. Fight the snake with the sword, and after slaying it, dismember it into seven pieces, which you should place on each step as you then ascend the pyramid.

At the top of the pyramid, approaching the bowl, you may meet a guide figure, who may be small and dressed in white, or made of metal. Allow your imagination to see who presides over the strange event you see in the bowl.

In the bowl you will see a vision of fire or water, or even both, in which bodies are being transformed from one form into another - death and rebirth in continual flux. Hear what the figure has to tell you about this vision. You may wish to read the following before engaging in this praxis:

> For all things are woven together and all things are taken apart and all things are mingled and all things combined and all things mixed and all things separated and all things are moistened and all things are dried and all things bud and all things blossom in the altar shaped like a bowl. For each, by method and by weight of the four elements, the interlacing and separation of the whole is accomplished for no bond can be made without method. The method is natural, breathing in and breathing out, keeping the orders of the method, increasing and decreasing. And all things by division and union come together in a harmony, the method not being neglected, the Nature is transformed. For the Nature, turning on itself, is changed. And the Nature is both the nature of the virtue and the bond of the world.

This is taken from the third century Greek alchemist, Zosimos of Panoplis, one of the very earliest writers on Alchemical transformation and vision. This praxis is based on the images that Zosimos dreamt so you are now recreating an experience that is almost two thousand years old. At this stage of the course, you may consider reading other alchemical visions or researching images, and creating your own *praxis* meditations.

If you build on the images introduced in this course, you will soon extend your range to experience a great many secrets of alchemy.

Once you have heard the guide explain the mysteries of the vision to you, ask him for your "writing tablet", which will be made of lead and which he will hand you. There may be a word written on this tablet which you should say out loud or write down in your physical body so that it is not forgotten. Thank the guide for this tablet, and take it with the sword down the pyramid. You may notice that something has happened to the dismembered parts of the snake as you descend.

Return to the Square of the Elements and again, you may find that it has been transformed to a more familiar and lively place. Place the Sword and Tablet in the Square, and return through the garden to the Gate of Vitriol.

Navigation Points

1. Create an Alchemical Body
2. Go through a Portal marked VITRIOL
3. Enter the Garden (deathly quiet)
4. Go the Square of the Elements (empty)
5. Find a Sword
6. Approach a Pyramid of Seven Steps
7. Slay & dismember the Serpent Guarding the Steps
8. Ascend the steps, placing each piece of the serpent on each step
9. Meet the Guide and see the Vision of the Bowl
10. Ask for and receive a lead writing tablet
11. Thank the figure and return

We have here reached the lowest and darkest part of our alchemical journey, the night before the dawn, which is the penultimate episode in this current course, and almost half-way through the twelve steps given by Ripley. Yet by mastering these lessons, you have achieved the first step in understanding putrefaction and death in Universe, and the deeper reality which informs all transformation. Here Ripley leaves us with this verse:

Now in this Chapter I have taught you,
How you must putrefy your body,
And so to guide you that you be not caught,
And put to durance loss and villany
My doctrine therefore remember wisely,
And pass forth towards the sixth gate,
For thus the fifth is triumphate.

Reading 5c (Source): The Dew of the Alchemists Garden

In our penultimate reading of source material, we will look at the work of Nicolas Flamel (1330 - 1417?) an alchemist of great repute and whose work here refers to the dew of alchemy, another important concept, particularly in plant alchemy, or *spagyric* alchemy. In this short extract, you might consider the Alchemical Garden; is it an actual garden, or an allegory?

For scans of Flamel's notebook, this link has excellent colour plates:

http://www.alchemylab.com/flameldwgs.htm

Extract from Flamel on Philosophy

And indeed the philosophers have a garden, where the sun as well morning as evening remains with a moist sweet dew, without ceasing, with which it is sprinkled and moistened; - whose earth brings forth trees and fruits, which are transplanted thither, which also receive descent and nourishment from the pleasant meadows. And this is done daily, and there they are both corroborated and quickened, without ever fading; and this more in one year, than in a thousand, where the cold affects them. - Take them therefore, and night and day cherish them in a distillatory fire; but not with a fire of wood or coals, but in a clear transparent fire, not unlike the sun, which is never hotter than is requisite, but is always alike; for a vapour is the dew, and seed of metals, which ought not to be altered.

Fruits, if they be too hot, and without dew or moisture, they abide on the boughs, but without coming to perfection, only withering or dwindling away. But if they be fed with heat and due moisture on their trees, then they prove elegant and fruitful; for heat and moisture are the elements of all earthly things, animal, vegetable, and mineral. Therefore fires of wood and coal produce or help not metals; those are violent fires, which nourish not as the heat of the sun does, that conserves all corporeal things; for that it is natural which they follow.

But a philosopher acts not what nature does; for nature where she rules, forms all vegetables, animals, and minerals, in their own degrees. Men, do not after the same sort, by their arts make natural things. When nature has finished her work about them; then by our art they are made more perfect. - In this manner the ancient sages and philosophers, for our information, wrought on luna and mercury her true mother, of which they made the mercury of the philosophers, which in its operation is much stronger than the natural mercury. For this is serviceable only to the simple, perfect, imperfect, hot and cold metals; but our mercury, the philosophers stone, is useful to the more than perfect, imperfect bodies, or metals. Also that the sun may perfect and nourish them without diminution, addition, or immutation, as they were created or formed by nature, and so leave them, not neglecting any thing.

Theoria V: Art and Alchemy

At this stage of your working through this six-month course, you are encouraged to prepare your own artwork based on the alchemical works you have now studied and experienced. This is a test of your approach to alchemy and your ability to work creatively and imaginatively with alchemy.

Again, you are encouraged to send your work at this stage to the author/mentor of this course for comment, if you would like feedback at this stage. It is suggested that your art-work is simple and from the heart, or perhaps your art may be to write your own praxis based on an alchemical text. Other suggestions include writing a poem, song or piece of music based on your appreciation of alchemy. You may also research how many other artists have found inspiration in alchemy and expressed the art in literature, popular music, and classic works.

Your work may be sent to adept@farawaycentre.com for feedback.

Module 6: Coagulation

In this final module, we will see how Alchemy has in itself been combined with other cosmologies, theories and approaches, particularly Kabbalah. Early writers on alchemy were not necessarily versed in other disciplines, and in some cases used terms interchangeably, or defined terms in their own particular ways. As alchemy moved through different cultures and across history, terms and translations were also subject to local interpretation.

It is important to keep returning to individual source works on alchemy in order to fully appreciate how it was seen by those who practiced it. It is useful - possibly essential - to understand their environment and culture. In a wider context it is important to know how certain terms were seen at that particular time; terms such as magic, spirit, and mind are all subject to differing meanings, particularly when they have been translated from Latin, or even European languages into English.

Coagulation means to "drive together" or "curdle"; it is the making of a thin liquid into a solid through a variety of processes. It is hoped that this course has assisted an inner coagulation of many thoughts and ideas into a reasonably fixed, stable, and solid appreciation of alchemy, from an introductory state! If you would like to continue coagulation, there are further avenues for discovery at the end of this course, and you may wish to contact me directly at the Far Away Centre.

Reading 6a (Academic): Kabbalah and Alchemy

By 1616, a degenerate form of Kabbalah as a generic term for elements of Alchemy had surfaced, as evidenced by the appearance of such works as Stephan Michelspacher, *Cabala, Spiegel der Kunst und Natur in Alchymia*. Augsburg, David Frank, 1616. This alchemical work, which is often reprinted, draws primarily from Agrippa's confused view of the Kabbalah and magic. The 'cabala' is referred to as 'mirror of Art and nature: in alchemy'.[115]

Gershom Scholem in his essay 'Alchemie und Kabbala'[116], demonstrated that there was no genuine Hebrew alchemical-kabbalistic tradition in the Renaissance: before the seventeenth century, Jewish Kabbalists were hardly interested in the pursuit of alchemy (Hayyim Vital in Safed being one of the exceptions, and then only briefly); nor did the alchemical symbolism of gold as the purest metal find any correlative in Kabbalistic symbolism. In this we discern a specific difference in the traditions, as symbolism is cultural and in the earliest forms of Alchemy and Kabbalah, development occurred in different cultural milieu's.

However, there were Jewish alchemists; 'kabbalistic alchemy' developed amongst Christian, not Jewish, alchemists as a result of the opening up of the hidden mysteries of the Kabbalah to the Christian scholarly world, according to Raphael Patai. Indeed, Patai states that the relationship between magic and alchemy is 'a field not yet investigated,' as 'the strictly orthodox alchemist would have nothing to do with magic'.[117]

Techne VI: Solve et Coagula

The final technical exercise of this course is based upon the idea of coagulation. It is also a wonderful party-trick and involves celebrating your completion of all the exercises and work these last six months. It should be done with the alcoholic material given below only if your local law permits you to purchase alcohol at your age, otherwise you should use the non-alcoholic equivalent.

The phrase *solve et coagula*; dissolve and solidify, comes from one of the few female alchemists to be held in high regard as a founding mother of alchemy; Maria Prophestissa, or Maria the Jewess. She was a 3rd Century alchemist and already a venerated historical figure when she was mentioned by Zosimos, who wrote the oldest recorded alchemical works in the 4th Century!

In this *techne* exercise, we will look at a pleasant way of experiencing *coagula*; in your *praxis* work of this module you will experience the *solve* aspect.

Materials

- Baileys Irish Cream (or Fresh Cream)
- Lime Juice

Experiment

This is an alchemical experiment you can taste, and is presented as a slightly light-hearted means of celebrating your conclusion of this six-month course. It is based on a cocktail called the 'cement-mixer' and is great to introduce at parties to a room full of people.

> Take a nice smooth shot of Baileys (or cream) but do not swallow it; rinse it around inside your mouth, like a mixer. Leave room for the second shot.
>
> Now take a shot of lime juice, swirling it around with the Baileys so you can enjoy the wonderful mixed taste you will experience.

You can let me know how much you enjoy this experiment.

There are many other ways in which you can experiment with *coagula*; for example, the freezing of water into ice or any other means of making a liquid solid is *coagula*.

Reading 6b (Source Material): A Work of Salt and Revelation

Many alchemical source materials are letters or diaries composed by the alchemists themselves. These were often in Latin or German, and many remain un-translated in large collections across the world. It was not until relatively recently that Issac Newton's writings on Alchemy were made publicly available. In fact, Issac Newton wrote more about alchemy than he did about science or gravity! In this extract, we will read a letter written in 1662, describing in detail an experiment with Salt, which was published in Thomas Vaughn's Lumen de Lumine.

Extract from A True Revelation (1662)

A TRUE REVELATION OF THE MANUAL OPERATION FOR THE UNIVERSAL MEDICINE COMMONLY CALLED 'THE PHILOSOPHER'S STONE b*y the celebrated philosopher of Leyden, as attested upon his deathbed with his own* Blood, Anno Domini 1662.

To my Loving Cousin and Son, the True Hermetic Philosopher--

Dear Loving Cousin and Son

Although I had resolved never to give in writing to any person the secret of the Ancient Sages, yet notwithstanding out of peculiar affection and love to you, I have taken it upon me, to which the nearness of our relation obliges me, and especially because this temporal life is short, and Art is very dark and you may therefore not attain the wished for end;--but my Son because so precious a jewel belongs not to swine; and also this so great a gift of God may be treated carefully and Christianlike, in consideration thereof I do so largely declare myself to thee.

I conjure thee with hand and mouth sacredly;

1st. That most especially thou faithfully keep the same from all wicked, lustful and criminal persons.

2dly. That thou exalt not thyself in any way.

3dly. That thou seek to advance the honor of thy Creator of all things and the good of thy neighbor, preserve it sacredly that thy Lord may not have cause to complain of thee at the last day. I have written here in this treatise such a part of the Kingdom of Heaven, just as I myself have worked this treasure and finished it with my fingers, therefore I have subscribed all this work with my blood, lying on my deathbed in Leyden.

THE PROCESS - In the Name of God, take of the purest and cleanest salt, sea salt, so as it is made by the sun itself, such as is brought by shipping from Spain, (I used salt that came from St. Uber) let it be dried in a warm stove, grind it in a stone mortar, as fine as possible to a powder that it may be so much the easier dissolve and taken up by our *Dew-water*, which is thus to be had in the months of May or June: When the Moon is at the full, observe when the dew falls with an East or South East wind. Then you must have sticks about one and a half feet high above the ground when driven in the Earth. Upon two or three such sticks, lay some four square plates of glass, and as the dew falls it easily fastens on the glass like a vapour, then have glass Vessels in readiness, let the dew drain from the sides of the glasses into your vessels. Do this until you have enough. The full of the Moon is a good season, afterwards it will be hard.

The solar rays descending from the sun carry with them solar sulphur--the Divine Fire. These rays are crystallized by contact with the lunar rays. The solar rays are also met by the emanations pouring upward from the earth's surface and are thus still further crystallized into a partly tangible substance, which is soluble in pure water. This substance is the "Magical Mountain of the Moon" referred to in the R. C. letter [see Reading 1c]. The crystallization of the solar and lunar rays in water (dew) produces the virgin earth--a pure, invisible substance, uncontaminated by material matter. When the virgin earth crystals are wet, they appear green; when dry, white.

Praxis VI

The Sixth Praxis - Congelation

Of Congelation I need not much to write,
But what it is, I will to you declare.
It is the induration of soft things of colour white,
And the fixation together of spirits which are flying ...

At last we come to the final meditation of this course; that of coagulation, or *congelatio*. This is the making of a solid from a liquid. It is also allegorical of the whole of creation; the manifestation of an apparent reality from an unknown source. In the idea of coagulation we see parallels to many forms of cosmology and philosophy that treat of an *emanative* system; one where a spiritualised reality becomes more tangible as it passes through various levels. In Kabbalah, this is depicted by the Tree of Life. One could also see this idea in the sequence of Tarot cards, from the unnumbered, limitless Fool card to the final card of the manifest and fixed World or Universe.

In this praxis we simplify the visualisation to create a coagulation of your learning on this whole course. Obviously, this exercise can only be done if you have accomplished the prior modules.

The Hall of Alchemical Memory

Enter into your Alchemical body and make your way through the Portal of Vitriol into the Square of the Elements. Search for - or ask directions - the Hall of Alchemy. Enter this Hall and find the hall of memory, which will be marked by a door or portal upon which is engraved **Solve et Coagula**. You now find yourself in an empty hall, which looks like an art gallery, although at present there are no pictures.

Find a bare wall which has room for three paintings. Stare at the wall in your imagination and follow the instructions below. You may need to read these several times before commencing this praxis, although they are straightforward in execution.

1. Think of the whole of the six-month alchemy course and notice the first thing that comes to mind where you had a "Aha!" or "Ummm...Fascinating!" feeling. Associate fully inside yourself and your memory of that event so that you recall what you saw and heard when you felt that feeling. Was it something you read, observed, thought about later, something someone said that clicked with an alchemical idea? An image in the course or a book?

2. Disassociate so you can create a picture of that moment. Freeze-frame it and hang it on the wall in the left position of the three parts of the wall. What sort of frame does the picture have?

3. Think of the whole course again and find another such learning moment. Associate fully again so you recall what you saw and heard when you felt that feeling. It may be similar or very different to the first.

4. Disassociate again so you can create a picture of that moment. Freeze-frame it and place it to the right of the first frame, in the centre position of the wall.

5. Repeat steps 1 & 2 a third time and place the framed picture to the right of the other two, so that you have three pictures on the wall - like frames in a movie.

6. Start to imagine that the pictures are now actually moving frames in a movie, running slowly at first, then faster and faster. They should start to blur together - this is the coagulation. Notice any emerging feeling from the movie – what is it that was underneath these three experiences, what is common, what is the overall lesson or communication you were receiving?

7. Allow yourself to wonder how you will act upon this meta-learning, and that you can use this technique in future for any course of learning or set of experiences.

This method - which comes from my training work in NLP (Neuro-Linguistic Programming) - often generates a semi-conscious "emergent pattern" which is only later realised, through a dream, a sudden positive behaviour which can be linked back to the learning, or a later "Ohhhh! I get it!" moment. So give it time to surface.

And finally...

Then is it named by Philosophers our starry stone,
Bring that to redness, then is the sixth gate won.

Reading 6c (General)

Conclusion: The Projection of the Stone

We have seen that Alchemy is an exemplar of the primary concerns and structure of the esoteric tradition, in its components as defined by Faivre. More recent writers have continued to use the mercurial nature of Alchemy to explore their own concerns, maintaining its significance as a universal construct or Rorshcach inkblot onto which the dynamic play of the psyche can be projected, much like the Stone itself was said to,

> A month having been completed, the omnipotent king or our stone arises, the perfect medicine of the third order in its projection able to transmute all metals.[118]

Heinrich (1995) considers the stone as an "ethneogenic substance (one that 'generates God' within a person)" in his chapter, Elixir: The Secret Stone of Alchemy.[119] In this he resumes the work of Allegro (1970) whose controversial work, *The Sacred Mushroom and the Cross*, speculated that Christianity was in essence developed from an Amanita-based pagan cult. In this, he is in the tradition of many other writers on the alchemy of hallucinogenics such as Lilly, Leary, and more recently McKenna and Pinchbeck, the latter of whom quotes the Anthropologist Alfred Metraux, "The shaman's power also has been described by some authorities as a substance which the magician carried in his body."[120] This substance is seen as the Alchemical elixir, by Pinchbeck and McKenna, and indeed the "complex symbols of alchemy are but one example of a property that seems to characterize mind in general; that is, its tendency to construct symbolic totality metaphors."[121]

In this, McKenna goes on to link the symbol of the Alchemical Monad, a synonym for the Lapis Philosophorum, with the holographic matrix, and mandala symbolism as a means for expressing the underlying order of psychic unity and totality. In this we can bridge between the neo-platonic and Aristotlean concerns of Alchemy and the philosophies of Leibniz – whose concept of plenum is as a "simple substance" like the Stone of the Wise and Whitehead's "extensive continuum."

Versluis examines the continued significance of alchemy in the writings of major 19th-century American writers who have drawn on the esoteric tradition, including Poe, Hawthorne, Melville, Emerson, Whitman, and Dickinson.[122] Whilst Hawthorne's *Scarlet Letter* may warn against alchemy, particularly herbalism, the concerns of the spiritual philosophy of alchemy are clearly voiced by Emerson, "every natural fact is a symbol of some spiritual fact."[123]

Indeed, Emerson's essay on Nature makes explicit the basis of the significance of alchemy in any enquiry;

> Man carries the world in his head – the whole astronomy and chemistry in a thought. Because the history of nature is characterised in his brain, therefore is he the prophet and discoverer of her secrets. Common sense knows its own, and recognises the fact at first sight in chemical experiment. The common sense of Franklin, Dalton, Davy, and Black, is the same common sense which made the arrangements it now discovers.[124]

The significance of Alchemy as a pictorial representation of spiritual seeking has continued in the realms of art. Although in the 16th and 17th centuries there were a number of artists who portrayed alchemy as a symbol of human folly, including Pieter Brueghel (c. 1525-69), David Teniers the Younger (1610-90), and Jan Steen (1626-79), surrealist artists and contemporary artists such as Anselm Kiefer[125] have, however, embraced the issues of alchemy in their works, maintaining alchemy as a significant communication of the esoteric spirit to a wider public; "For Kiefer the alchemist, the world is a physical entity, requiring a philosophy in which reflection and action are joined."[126]

Alchemy has also been applied to the role of the feminine archetype in mysticism[127], and esoteric sexual practices, with analysis of the soror mystica, Sophia, and Anima Mundi. In *The Golden Age Restored*, erotic allegories are inserted from The Song of Songs; "My Beloved is white and ruddy, the chiefest amongst ten thousand. His head is as the most fine gold, his locks are bushy, and black as a raven."[128]

However, the Stone remains elusive[129];

> Alchemist: They say true when they call you a wonderful and inconstant and volatile substance.
>
> Mercury: You call me inconstant. But to the constant I am also constant, and to the man of fixed resolve, I am fixed.

The nature of the Stone is central to our dilemma as students of the esoteric tradition; it is both quest and destination, both ourselves and other, tool and product, it is the eye that observes and cannot see itself, knowing itself through exhaustion of all possibilities through experiment. It is indeed, the mystery of awareness.

Jung came to call Mercurius, the 'paradox par excellence.' Our frustration with alchemy is not new; in desperation for understanding, when the alchemist of *The New Chemical Light* calls on divine invocations to subdue his subject, Mercury, the substance becomes apparently weak and obsequious. The alchemist, rightly suspecting more elusiveness, speaks plainly and questions Mercury, whose answer states the nature of our dilemma examining the *ars alchimica*,

Alchemist: What is the matter with you?

Mercury: An Alchemist is the matter with me. [130]

Theoria VI: Beyond the Six Gates

As you come at last to the final portal of this amphitheatre, you may rest assured you have travelled far and wondered often. The alchemy of transformation does not rest, it is indeed an eternal stone, working miracles in front of our very eyes, but we have only awakened a little to see such vision.

The Theoria work of this last gate is to encourage you to research and work further in many of the related avenues to alchemy, whether it be through Kabbalah, Herb-Lore, History or Chemistry. Did you know that Issac Newton wrote more about Alchemy than he did about Gravity? His alchemical notes are now available on-line:

http://webapp1.dlib.indiana.edu/newton/index.jsp

To explore the history of chemistry and alchemy, you may wish to join the Society for the History of Alchemy and Chemistry and subscribe to their journal, AMBIX:

http://www.ambix.org/

Bibliography and Reading List

Agrippa, Henry Cornelius, *Three Books of Occult Philosophy* (trans. James Freake) (St Paul: Llewellyn, 1998)

Barrett, Francis, *The Magus* (Secaucus: Citadel Press, 1980)

Beitchman, Philip, *Alchemy of the Word: Cabala of the Renaissance* (Albany: State University of New York Press, 1998)

Broek, Roelof van den and Hanegraaff, Wouter J. (ed.), *Gnosis and Hermeticism* (New York: State University of New York Press, 1998)

Copenhaver, Brian P. (trans.), *Hermetica* (Cambridge: Cambridge University Press, 1992)

de Rola, Stanislas K., *The Golden Game: Alchemical Engravings of the Seventeenth Century* (London: Thames & Hudson, 1988)

Eranos Jahrbuch (46) 1977

Faivre, Antoine, *Access to Western Esotericism* (New York: State University of New York Press, 1994)

Gilly, Carlos, *Magic, Alchemy and Science 15th-18th Centuries: The Influence of Hermes Trismegistus* (Amsterdam: Bibliotheca Philosophica Hermetica, 2002)

Hames, Harvey J., *The Art of Conversion: Christianity and Kabbalah in the Thirteenth Century* (Leiden: Brill, 2000)

Idel, Moshe, *Kabbalah, New Perspectives* (New Haven: Yale University Press, 1988)

Kaplan, Stewart, *Encyclopaedia of Tarot, Vol. III*

Levi, Eliphas, (trans. A. E. Waite) *The History of Magic* (London: Rider, 1982)

Levi, Eliphas, *The Book of Splendours* (Wellinborough: The Aquarian press, 1983)

Levi, Eliphas, *Transcendental Magic: Its Doctrine and Ritual* (1910) (Kessinger, 2006)

Linden, Stanton J., *The Alchemy Reader* (Cambridge: Cambridge University Press, 2003)

Mclean, Adam, *The Western Mandala* (Edinburgh: Hermetic Research Series, 1983)

Mead, G. S., Fragments of a Faith Forgotten (New York: New Hyde Park, 1960)

Miller, Paul J.W., 'Introduction' in Wallis, Miller & Carmichael, *Pico della Mirandola: On the Dignity of Man* (Indianapolis: Hackett Publishing, 1998)

Patai, Raphael, *The Jewish Alchemists* (Princeton: Princeton University Press, 1994)

Petrement, Simon, A Separate God: The Origins and teachings of Gnosticism (New York: Haper Collins, 1984)

Prinke, Rafal T., 'Lampado Trado', in *The Hermetic Journal*, 30 (1985)

Redgrove, H. Stanley, *Alchemy: Ancient and Modern* (Wakefield: EP Publishing Ltd, 1973)

Scholem, Gershom G., *Kabbalah* (New York: Dorset Press, 1974)

Scholem, Gershom G., *Major Trends in Jewish Mysticism* (New York: Schocken Books, 1961)

Stuckrad, Kocku von, Western Esotericism (London: Equinox Publishing Ltd, 2005)

Wallis, Miller & Carmichael, *Pico della Mirandola: On the Dignity of Man* (Indianapolis: Hackett Publishing, 1998)

Yates, Frances, *The Rosicrucian Enlightenment* (St Albans: Granada, 1975)

Notes

[1] Dion Fortune, *The Mystical Qabalah* (London & Tonbridge: Ernest Benn Limited, 1979), pp.1-7. Although often misquoted or misattributed, it was Dion Fortune who referred to Qabalah providing a basis for the practical work of the "Yoga of the West," in her introduction to *The Mystical Qabalah*. However, it is a *particular* Yoga – she later refers to individuals within the Church developing their own mystical tradition, akin to Bhakti Yoga.

[2] Vishwas Vasant Mandlik, 'Classification, Levels and method of mastering the Asanas', *Yoga Point*, <http://www.yogapoint.com/info/article10.htm> [accessed 26 December 2005] (para. 2 of 21).

[3] Charles D. Laughlin, 'Transpersonal Anthropology, Then and Now', *Lila: Journal of Cosmic Play* [n.d]
<http://www.lila.info/document_view.phtml?document_id=49> [accessed 26 December 2005] (para. 16 of 23). See also the work of Ken Wilbur, 'Excerpt D: The Look of a Feeling: The Importance of Post/Structuralism', *Part IV. Conclusions of Adequate Structuralism* [n.d]
<http://wilber.shambhala.com/html/books/kosmos/excerptD/part4-4.cfm> [accessed 26 December 2005] (paras. 12-13 of 33). *Polyphasic* cultures value different states of consciousness as part of the cultural identity, whereas *monophasic* cultures and societies sanction only one or two states, i.e. waking and sleeping.

[4] Antoine Faivre, *Access to Modern Esotericism* (Albany: State University of New York Press, 1994), p. 46.

[5] James Lett, 'Emic/Etic Distinctions', *Encyclopedia of Cultural Anthropology* (1996)
<http://faculty.ircc.cc.fl.us/faculty/jlett/Article%20on%20Emics%20and%20Etics.htm> [accessed 26 December 2005] (para. 8 of 10). An *etic* construct is correctly termed *etic* if and only if it is in accord with the epistemological principles deemed appropriate by science (i.e., etic constructs must be precise, logical, comprehensive, replicable, falsifiable, and observer independent).

[6] Faivre, p.163

[7] Paul Brunton, *The Hidden Teachings Beyond Yoga* (London: Rider, 1941). Brunton makes the case for a hybrid approach to mysticism combining the elements of Yoga with the 'sensibilities' of the West. He points out that the stilling of the mind from Asana and Yoga practices is merely useful preparation for thought, not a goal in itself.

[8] Mandlik, para. 2 of 21.

[9] Edward F. Edinger, *Anatomy of the Psyche: Alchemical Symbolism in Psychotherapy* (Illinois: Open Court Press, 1994), p. 2. This is quoted from Jung, CW 14, para. 792, but Edinger's book gives a clearer depiction of the stages of alchemy corresponding to the individuation process, and hence, to some degree, the initiation system of the esoteric tradition.

[10] Caitlin and John Matthews, *The Western Way*, 2 vols (London: Arkana, 1986), II, 199-231 (pp. 202-3). The Matthews consider alchemy as a microcosm of the Western Way in its descent, arising from native cosmological speculations, receiving the influx of Gnosticism, Philosophy (one assumes both Aristotlean and Platonic), and multifarious Middle Eastern sources, to become a powerful tradition in its own right. They also forge the link of the Alchemist to the Smith archetype, as Wayland or Hephaistos, as expanded by Eliade in *The Forge and the Crucible*. The Alchemist is in effect a precursor or parallel to the Mason – a tool-user imbued by the mystery of his knowledge and ability to construct and deconstruct.

[11] Charles Poncé, *Alchemy: Papers Towards a Radical Metaphysics* (North Atlantic Books, 1983)

[12] Quoted in Carl Henrich, *Strange Fruit* (London: Bloomsbury, 1995), p. 40. Originally from Norton, Theatr. Chem. 'Ordinall' p. 40.

[13] Adam Mclean, *Commentary on the Chymical Wedding*, Magnum Opus Hermetic Sourceworks No.18 (Edinburgh: Hermetic Research Trust, 1984), p. 110.

[14] Cherry Gilchrist, *The Elements of Alchemy* (Dorset: Element, 1998), p.7.

[15] Quoted in Frater Albertus, *The Alchemist's Handbook* (Maine:Weiser, 1974), p. 6.

[16] Herwig Buntz, Alchemy III: $12^{th}/13^{th}$-15th Century, in *Dictionary of Gnosis & Western Esotericism* [Hereafter DGWE] 2 vols (Boston: Brill, 2005), I, 36.

[17] Wouter J. Hanegraaff, New Age Religion and Western Culture (Leiden: Brill, 1996), pp. 395-5. This chapter also contains useful reference sources for the historical argument.

[18] Quoted in William R. Newman, *Promethean Ambitions* (Chicago: University of Chicago Press, 2004), p.117 which also discusses the tensions inherent in the 'Neoplatonizing Aristotelianism of medieval and early modern natural philosophy'.

[19] Jon Marshall, The Emerald Tablet of Hermes, The Alchemy Website [n.d.] <http://www.alchemywebsite.com/emerald.html> [accessed 26 December 2005] originally from B.J. Dobbs, 'Newton's Commentary on the Emerald

Tablet of Hermes Trismegistus' in Merkel, I and Debus A.G. *Hermeticism and the Renaissance* (Washington: Folger, 1988).

[20] Macbeth, Act I, Scene III

[21] The Tempest , Act IV, Scene I

[22] Antoine Faivre, 'Renaissance Hermeticism and the Concept of Western Esotericism' in *Gnosis and Hermeticism from Antiquity to Modern Times*, ed. by Roelof van den Broek and Wouter J. Hanegraaff (New York: State University of New York Press, 1998), pp.119-20.

[23] Stanton J. Linden, *The Alchemy Reader* (Cambridge: Cambridge University Press, 2003) p. 4

[24] John Read, *From Alchemy to Chemistry* (New York: Dover Publications, 1995) p. 74

[25] Mircea Eliade, *The Forge and the Crucible* (Chicago: University of Chicago Press, 1978) pp. 79-96

[26] Elias Ashmole, *Theatrum chemicum britannicum : containing severall poeticall pieces of our famous English philosophers, who have written the hermetique mysteries in their owne ancient language* (London : Printed by J. Grismond for Nath: Brooke, at the angel in Cornhill, 1652). In *Edgar Fahs Smith Memorial Collection.* QD25 .A78. p. A2r [http://dewey.library.upenn.edu/sceti/printedbooksNew/index.cfm?TextID=ashmole&PagePosition=1 , last accessed 16 May 2007]

[27] Thomas Tymme, *The Practise of Chymicall, and Hermetic Physicke* (London, 1605), quoted in Linden, *ibid*, p. 5

[28] Charles Mackay, *Extraordinary Popular Delusions and the Madness of Crowds* (New York: Harmony Books, 1980), p. 100

[29] James Webb, *The Flight from Reason* (London: Macdonald, 1971) p. 139

[30] Antoine Faivre, *Access to Western Esotericism* (Albany: State University of New York Press, 1994) pp. 68 - 9

[31] Wouter J. Hanegraaff (ed.), *Dictionary of Gnosis and Western Esotericism Vol. I* (Leiden: Brill, 2005) pp. 12-14. See this section for a discussion of the popularisation of the 'psychological' or 'spiritual' elements of alchemy in the 19th century through the work of Mary Anne Atwood, *Suggestive Inquiry into the Hermetic Mystery* (1850).

[32] Nicholas Goodrick-Clarke, *Paracelsus: Essential Readings* (Wellingborough: Crucible, 1990) p. 33

[33] Paracelsus, *de Natura rerum* (1537) I/11, pp. 348-9 of Karl Sudhoff & Wilhelm Matthiessen (eds.) *Paracelsus, Samtliche Werke* (Munich: O. W. Barth, 1922-25) quoted in Jolande jacobi (ed.) *Paracelsus: Selected Writings* (New Jersey: Princetown University Press, 1979) pp. 141 - 3

[34] http://www.levity.com/alchemy/ripgat1.html

[35] E. F. Edinger, *Anatomy of the Psyche* (Chicago: Open Court, 1994) pp. 42-3

[36] Ripley, *Ibid*.

[37] Adam Mclean, *The Western Mandala*, Hermetic Research Series No.3 (Edinburgh: Hermetic Research Trust, 1983), pp. 1-3.

[38] Iain McCalman, *The Last Alchemist* (New York: Perennial, 2004), pp.164-68.

[39] HYLE - International Journal for Philosophy of Chemistry, Vol. 9, No.2 (2003), pp. 131-70.

[40] Aleister Crowley, *Magick* (London: Routledge & Kegan Paul, 1973), p. 263.

[41] A meditative practice by which the practitioner seeks to create a 'Body of Light' or 'Astral Body' which is then projected into a series of hierarchically organised 'planes' of existence, each of which has its own qualities. This self-guided visualisation was termed 'Rising on the Planes' primarily by the Golden Dawn.

[42] Crowley, p. 263.

[43] Peter Gabriel, *Here Comes the Flood* (1977)

[44] Richard Cavendish, *The Black Arts* (London: Pan, 1967) p. 182

[45] C. G. Jung, CW 14, p. 160

[46] James Hillman, "Therapeutic Value of Alchemical Language", in *Dragonflies: Studies in Imaginal Psychology, Vol.1. No.1.* p. 37

[47] *The Fountain of the Lovers of the Science*, composed by John Fountain of Valencienn in the County of Hainault. Lyons 1590. (MS. Sloane 3637 in the British Library), available trans. Adam Mclean:
http://www.alchemywebsite.com/johnfont.html
[Last Accessed 17 May 2007]

[48] Stanislas Klossowski de Rola, *Steganographic Collection*, translation of "*Le Tableau des Riches Inventions: Couvertes du voile des feintes Amoureuses, qui sont representees dans le Songe de Poliphile Desvoilees des ombres du Songe & subtilement exposees par Beroalde. A Paris Chez Matthieu Guillemot, au Palais en la galerie des prisonniers. Avec privilege du Roy. 1600*":
http://www.alchemywebsite.com/beroalde.html
[Last Accessed 17 May 2007]

[49] http://www.levity.com/alchemy/rosdesc.html
[Last Accessed 20 May 2007]

[50] C. G. Jung, CW 16, p. 200

[51] C. G. Jung, CW 12, p. 331

[52] C. G. Jung, CW 13, p.69

[53] Karen-Claire Voss, *The Hierosgamos Theme in the Images of the Rosarium Philosophorum* in *Alchemy Revisited: Proceedings of the International Conference on the History of Alchemy at the University of Groningen, 17-19 April 1989*, ed. by Z.R.W.M. von Martels (Leiden: E.J. Brill, 1990):
http://www.istanbul-yes-istanbul.co.uk/alchemy/Rosariumfinal.htm
[Last accessed 17 May 2007].

[54] Julian Huxley, 'The Coming New Religion of Humanism' in *Is Secular Humanism a Religion?* [n.d.]

<http://members.aol.com/VFTfiles/Humanism/huxley.htm> [accessed 26 December 2005] originally printed in *The Humanist* (January/February 1962).

[55] Michael Talbot, *Mysticism and the New Physics* (London: Routledge & Kegan Paul, 1981), Chapter 1:Observer and Participant.

[56] Louise B. Young, *The Unfinished Universe* (New York: Simon and Schuster, 1986) which is subtitled, 'a radical new view that the universe is perfecting itself.'

[57] Newman, p. 29.

[58] Indeed, the cover of New Scientist (3rd July 2004) and Eliade's *The Forge and the Crucible* (Chicago: University of Chicago Press, 1978) share almost identical cover designs, and the issues discussed in Eliade's title, 'the origins and structures of alchemy,' are mirrored in the New Scientist cover taglines, "Pentaquark: A riddle at the root of Reality," and "The Immortality Factor."

[59] Carlos Gilly, 'The Amphitheatrum Sapientiae Aeternae of Heinrich Khunrath' in *Magic, Alchemy and Science 15th-18th Centuries: The Influence of Hermes Trismegistus* (Amsterdam: Bibliotheca Philosophica Hermetica, 2002) p. 225

[60] The *Amphitheatrum* also derives from the compendium, "Artis cabbalisticæ, h. e. reconditæ theologiæ et philosophiæ scriptorum tomus unus" (Basle, 1587) published by Pistorius (1546-1608) a controversialist and historian.

[61] Ibid, annot. 230, p. 342

[62] Robert Turner (trans.) *Arbatel of Magick* (1655) p. 2. The Arbatel also talks of eight kinds of Magic, ranging from Microcosmical Magic to Prophetical Magic.

[63] Ibid, annot. 43, p. 342

[64] Ibid, p. 345

[65] F. Sherwood Taylor, *The Alchemists* (London: The Scientific Book Club, [n.d.]), p. 142.

[66] Richard Cavendish, *The Black Arts* (London: Pan Books, 1967) p.180-97. This book is titled for sensational value only, and the chapter on 'The Making of the Stone,' remains one of the few practical interpretations of alchemical processes in the context of the initiatory process in publication. However, there is now a more recent analysis - from a Jungian point of view - Edinger's *Anatomy of the Psyche*.

[67] Faivre, *Access*, p.170.

[68] Stephan A. Hoeller, 'C.G. Jung and the Alchemical Renewal', *Gnosis*, 8 (1998), pp. 34-9.

[69] A.E. Waite, *Alchemists through the Ages* (New York: Rudolph Steiner Publications, 1970), p. 13.

[70] DGWE, p. 46.

[71] Jim Melodini, 'The Age of Gold', *Gnosis*, 8 (1998), pp. 8-10.

[72] Israel Regardie, *The Golden Dawn*, 6th edn. (St Paul, MN: Llewellyn, 1989) Adeptus Minor Ritual, p. 228.

[73] Mircea Eliade, *The Forge and the Crucible*, 2nd edn. (Chicago: University of Chicago press, 1978), p. 190.

[74] C.G. Jung, trans. R.F.C. Hull, *Alchemical Studies* (London: Routledge & Kegan Paul, 1967), p. 123.

[75] http://en.wikipedia.org/wiki/Cesare_Ripa also http://emblem.libraries.psu.edu/Ripa/Images/ripatoc.htm for all the emblems and translated text.

[76] S. Kaplan, *The Encyclopaedia of Tarot* (New York: US Games Systems, Inc, 1978) pp. 36-8

[77] http://www.levity.com/alchemy/amcl_beccafumi.html [Last Accessed 20 May 2007]

[78] Adam Mclean, 'The Fourth Rosicrucian Manifesto? The Mirror of Wisdom of Theophilus Schweighardt' in *The Hermetic Journal 25* (Edinburgh, Autumn 1984), illus. p. 26, p. 32

[79] *Ibid*, p. 31

[80] Allison Coudert, *Alchemy: The Philosopher's Stone* (Boulder: Shambala, 1980) pp. 91-2

[81] Nicholas Barnaud, The Book of Lambspring (1599). Lucas Jennis, *Dyas chymica tripartita* (1625), http://www.levity.com/alchemy/lambsprg.html [Last accessed 17 may 2007]

[82] Royston M. Roberts, *Serendipity: Accidental Discoveries in Science* (New York: Wiley, 1989) pp. 75-81

[83] C. G. Jung, ed by Aniela Jaffe, transl. by R. & C. Winston, *Memories, Dreams, Reflections* (Vintage, 1963) p. 200

[84] Joseph. L. Henderson & Dyane N. Sherwood, *Transformation of the Psyche: The Symbolic Alchemy of the Splendor Solis* (Hove: Routledge, 2003) p. 1

[85] C. G. Jung, *Psychology and Alchemy* (London: Routledge, 1989) & *Alchemical Studies* (New Jersey: Routledge & Kegan Paul, 1983). Also referred to as CW 12 & CW 13.

[86] C. G. Jung, CW 12, p. 282-3

[87] Karen Claire-Voss, 'Imagination in Mysticism and Esotericism: Marsillio Ficino, Ignatius de Loyola, and Alchemy' in *Studies in Spirituality* No. 6 (1996) pp. 106-30

[88] See Joseph. L. Henderson & Dyane N. Sherwood, *Transformation of the Psyche: The Symbolic Alchemy of the Splendor Solis* (Hove: Routledge, 2003),

Edward. F. Edinger, *Anatomy of the Psyche: Alchemical Symbolism in Psychotherapy* (Chicago & La Salle: Open Court, 1994), Marie-Louise von Franz, *Alchemical Active Imagination* (Boston: Shamballa, 1979), and Jeffrey Raff, *Jung and the Alchemical Imagination* (Nicolas-Hayes, 2003)

[89] C. G. Jung, CW 13, p. 199

[90] Herbert Silberer, *Hidden Symbolism of Alchemy and the Occult Arts* (New York: Dover, 1971) pp. 112-45 (originally published 1917) where Silberer notes that "the alchemists like to dwell on the process of procreation, and on infantile sexual theories...", surveys the comparison of the alchemical *prima materia* to spittle and other "secretions and excretions" and ponders on the creation of the *homunculus*.

[91] http://www.levity.com/alchemy/parabola.html [last accessed 17 May 2007]

[92] For discussion on the authorship and name of the author, cf. http://www.lohengrin-verlag.de/Rosenkreutz/Rosenkreuzer.htm (German) [last accessed 17 May 2007]

[93] Herbert Silberer, *Problems of Mysticism and its Symbolism* (Kessinger, 2003) pp. 19 - 22 [originally published 1914].

[94] Silberer, *ibid*, p. 21

[95] For the influence - or otherwise - of the philosophical perspectives of *Naturphilosophie* on Jung, cf. Richard Noll, *The Jung Cult* (London: Fontana, 1996), p. 42.

[96] B. J. Gibbons, *Spirituality and the Occult* (London: Routledge, 2001) p.104

[97] *Ibid*, p. 106. Note also that Schubert wrote *Die Symbolik des Traumes* in 1814, pre-figuring Freud's own work on the subject of dreams, and Jung's on Symbolism.

[98] C. G. Jung, CW 12, pp. 315-6

[99] Walter Pagel, 'Jungs Views on Alchemy', in *Isis*, Vol. 39, No. ½. (May, 1948), pp. 44-8

[100] DGWE, II, p. 1009

[101] Christopher McIntosh, *The Rosicrucians* (Wellingborough: Crucible, 1987), p. 46

[102] http://en.wikipedia.org/wiki/Image:Andportraits2.jpg, last accessed 29th September 2006

[103] Carlos Gilly, *Theophrastia Sanca: Paracelsianism as a religion in conflict with the established churches* at: http://www.ritmanlibrary.nl/c/p/res/art/art_01.html, last accessed 27 September 2006, IV & note 41.

[104] C. G. Jung, CW 12, p. 252-4

[105] C. G. Jung, CW 13, p. 88

[106] Zosimos of Panopolis, *Of Virtue, Lessons 1-3* (fl. C. 300AD) quoted in Linden, *ibid*, p. 51

[107] J. V. Andreae, *The Chymical Wedding of Christian Rosenkreutz* (Strasbourg, 1616) translated by E. Foxcroft (1690) presented in Gareth Knight & Adam Mclean, *Commentary on the Chymical Wedding* (Edinburgh: Magnum Opus, 1984) p. 12

[108] John Datin's Dream in Elias Ashmole's *Theatrum Chemicum Britannicum.* Transcribed by Justin von Bujdoss:
http://www.alchemywebsite.com/tcbdastn.html
[Last Accessed 17 May 2007]

Elias Ashmole, *Theatrum Chemicum Britannicum. Containing Severall Poetical Pieces of our Famous English Philosophers, who have written the Hermetique Mysteries in their owne Ancient Language. Faithfully Collected into one Volume, with Annotations thereon, by Elias Ashmole, Esq. Qui est Mercuriophilus Anglicus. The first part, London, Printed by J. Grismond for Nath: Brooke, at the Angel in Cornhill. MDCLII. 1652.*

[109] http://en.wikipedia.org/wiki/Hypnagogia

[110] A. Mavromatis, *Hypnagogia: the Unique State of Consciousness Between Wakefulness and Sleep.* (London: Routledge and Kegan Paul, 1987)

[111] Simon J. Sherwood, *Relationship between the hypnagogic/hypnopompic states and reports of anomalous experiences,* Department of Psychology, The University of Edinburgh:
http://www.geocities.com/soho/gallery/3549/pa_sp3.html
[Last Accessed 17 May 2007]

[112] *The Golden Age Restored* in Johann Grasshof, *Dyas chymica tripartita...* (Frankfurt, 1625), ascribed to Henricus Madathanus, a pseudonym of Hadrian à Mynsicht:
http://www.alchemywebsite.com/goldnage.html
[Last Accessed 17 May 2007]

[113] Adam McLean (editor), Patricia Tahil (translator) *The Hermetic Garden of Daniel Stolcius* (1980)

[114] Linden, *ibid*, p. 51

[115] Steffan Michelspacher, *Cabala* (1616) in Stanislas K. de Rola, *The Golden Game: Alchemical Engravings of the Seventeenth Century* (London: Thames & Hudson, 1988) p. 52 (text) & p. pp. 54-5 (images).

[116] *Eranos* Jahrbuch (46) 1977, pp. 1-96

[117] Raphael Patai, *The Jewish Alchemists* (Princeton: Princeton University Press, 1994) p. 6

[118] Quoted from the *Cabala Mineralis*, a 17th century emblematic alchemy work, discussed by Adam Mclean in answer to a question in the Alchemical Academy (September 2004), <http://www.alchemywebsite.com/a-archive_sep04.html> [accessed 26 December 2005]. The work in question raises several important points about the vagaries of attribution, dating, and interpretation of such documents, in this case to the purported linkage of Kabbalah and Alchemy that can be derived from the emblems and authorship.

[119] Carl Henrich, *Strange Fruit* (London: Bloomsbury, 1995), p.163. An unusual book which purports that the stone was not, as assumed by 'most investigators' to be a 'psychic experience' but rather the fly agaric mushroom.

[120] Quoted in Daniel Pinchbeck, *Breaking Open the Head* (London: Flamingo, 2003), p.71.

[121] Terence McKenna and Daniel McKenna, *The Invisible Landscape* (New York: HarperCollins, 1993), p.51.

[122] Arthur Versluis, *The Esoteric Origins of the American Renaissance* (Oxford & New York: Oxford U P, 2001).

[123] Ralph Waldo Emerson, *Nature*, in Essays of Ralph Waldo Emerson, (London: J.M. Dent & Sons, 1934), p. 302.

[124] *Ibid*, p. 302.

[125] Nicolas Pioch, 'Anselm Kiefer', WebMuseum, Paris.
<http://www.ibiblio.org/wm/paint/auth/kiefer/> [accessed 26 December 2005].

[126] Mark Rosenthal, *Anselm Kiefer* (Prestel Publishing, 1998).

[127] Poncé, 'Woman, the Feminine and Alchemy', p.73-89.

[128] Quoted in Wayne Shumaker, *The Occult Sciences in the Renaissance* (London: University of California Press, 1979), p. 190.

[129] Michael Sendivogius, 'The New Chemical Light', in *Concerning the Secrets of Alchemy and other tracts from the Hermetic Museum* (Llanerch Enterprises, 1989), p. 138.

[130] *Ibid*, p.135.

A

A.E. Waite 67
Adelard of Bath 18
Air 29, 30, 64, 68, 75
albedo 81, 105
Alchemical Adoration of the Evening
.... 76
Alchemical Adoration of the Morning
.... 75
Alchemical Adorations 74
Alchemical Body 28, 30, 106, 107
Alchemical Garden 29, 44, 85, 106, 108
Alchemical Monad 119
Alchemist 10, 12, 13, 16, 25, 26, 32, 33, 52, 102, 105, 120, 121
Alchemy . 1, 3, 4, 6, 7, 8, 9, 10, 11, 13, 15, 16, 17, 18, 22, 23, 24, 26, 27, 31, 32, 36, 39, 47, 51, 52, 57, 58, 59, 64, 67, 75, 76, 77, 79, 81, 92, 96, 102, 110, 111, 112, 114, 117, 119, 120, 122, 123, 124
Aleister Crowley 20, 30, 62
AMORC 83
Amphitheatre 1, 6, 43, 54, 77, 85
Andreae .... 83, 89, 92, *See* Rosicrucian
anima 49
animus 49
apprenticeship 4
Arbatel 54
Asana 15, 22, 24, 125

B

Basil Valentine 26, 39, 66, 67, 81
Bird of Hermes 67
Bonus of Ferrara 17
Book of Lambspring 78, 95
Book of the Composition of Alchemy 18

C

Calcination 5, 14, 27, 31, 46, 58, 82
Carl Gustav Carus 80
Cauda Pavonis 105
Cesare Ripa 74
Chaldean Oracles 98
Chymical Wedding 16, 83, 84, 89
Chymical Wedding' 16
Cibation 58
Coagulation 5, 111
Confessio Fraternitatis 83
Congelation 27, 58, 116
Conjunction 5, 27, 58, 63, 64, 69, 82
correspondences 22, 59, 79, 80
Cosmology 16
Crowning of Nature 64

D

dew 75, 97, 108, 109, 115
Divine Pymander 20

Domenico Beccafumi 77
dreams 30, 47, 49, 78, 80, 92

E

Earth 29, 30, 64, 68, 75, 115
Exaltation 58

F

Faivre 15, 22, 23, 39, 58, 59, 79, 119, 123, 125
Fama Fraternitatis 83
Far Away Centre 4, 8, 9, 111
Fermentation 58
Fire ... 13, 23, 29, 30, 32, 33, 62, 64, 65, 68, 75, 115

G

George Ripley 18, 27, 58
Gershom Scholem 112
Golden Age Restored 93, 120
Great Work 16, 67
Guide . 4, 32, 33, 34, 35, 45, 46, 62, 63, 85, 95, 107

H

Harpocrates 20
Heinrich Khunrath 77
Herbert Silberer 79, 92
Hermes Trismegestus 94
Hermes Trismegistus 52, 55, 123
Hermetic Garden 94, 103
Hermetic Order of the Golden Dawn 66
Hermeticism 16, 36, 58, 123
hypnagogic 79, 92, 93, 94

I

IAO 91
initiations 69

J

James Hillman 47
Janus 82
John of the Fountain 47
Jung . 10, 15, 23, 47, 48, 49, 59, 79, 80, 92, 93, 121

K

Kabbalah ... 4, 8, 9, 15, 41, 54, 62, 81, 82, 111, 112, 116, 122, 123, 124
Kekulé 78
Khunrath 54, 55, 77, 92
King and Queen 49, 82

L

Lapis Philosophorum 119
Le Tableau des Riches Inventions 48
Learned and Christian Society 83
Lumen de Lumine 34, 114

M

Magick 4, 54
Magicka School 4, 9
Maria Prophestissa 113
Mercury 7, 24, 44, 45, 52, 61, 62, 63, 67, 81, 82, 96, 100, 120, 121
Michael Maier 26, 47
Moon 32, 33, 37, 38, 44, 67, 93, 98, 115
Multiplication 58
Mutus Liber 81

N

Naturphilosophie 18, 58
Neptune 82
Nicolas Flamel 108
nigredo 81, 105
NLP 4, 118

P

Parabola of Madathanus 79
Paracelsus 6, 23, 83, 102
Paragranum 102
Parcelsus 52
Petrus Bonus 18
Philosopher's Stone 10, 54, 57, 81
Philosophia Reformata 26, 27, 93
Projection 58, 119
Psychotherapists 79
putrefaction 91, 102, 105, 107
Putrefaction 5, 27, 58, 81, 91, 105

R

Reformation 59
Regardie 60, 91
ritual 10, 20, 39, 52, 56, 59, 96
Ritual 4, 8, 96, 97, 123
Roger Bacon 18
Rosarium Philosophorum 48, 50
Rosicrucian 69, 83, 124
Rosicrucians 16, 77
rubedo 81, 105

S

Salt . 1, 7, 24, 40, 56, 61, 62, 63, 64, 81, 82, 96, 98, 100, 114
Schrondingers Cat 51
Separation 5, 27, 53, 58, 61, 63
Shakespeare 21
Sigils 20
Solution 5, 27, 38, 44, 45, 46, 58, 61, 82
Solve et Coagula 113, 117
Spagyric 10
Square of the Elements 32, 33, 44, 62, 85, 106, 107, 117
String Theory 52
Sublimation 58
Sulpher 6, 7, 24, 61, 62, 63, 66, 81, 82, 96, 100
Sun 32, 33, 37, 45, 49, 65, 67, 86, 89, 93, 98

T

Tarot ... 4, 8, 9, 20, 38, 44, 74, 85, 86, 91, 116, 123
Teilhard de Chardin 52
The Age of Gold 59
The Alchemical Wedding 92
The Chemical Wedding 70
The Emerald Tablet 19, 36, 37
The Stairway of the Wise 24
theurgy 52
Three Principles 62
transformation .. 10, 14, 20, 24, 38, 39, 58, 59, 61, 63, 69, 77, 102, 105, 106, 107, 122

V

Varjayana 16
VITRIOL 15, 29, 30, 107
Vulcan 23, 102, 103, 104

W

Water 29, 30, 44, 45, 46, 56, 64, 68, 75, 82, 98
Witchcraft 4, 8, 9

Z

Zosimos 52, 59, 92, 95, 106, 113
Zosimos of Panoplis 106

www.ingramcontent.com/pod-product-compliance
Ingram Content Group UK Ltd.
Pitfield, Milton Keynes, MK11 3LW, UK
UKHW051524180426
11947UKWH00018B/1560